ESSENTIAL
History of
ART

Acknowledgements

This book has been made possible by four authors: Lucinda Hawksley, Antonia Cunningham, Laura Payne and Kirsten Bradbury. They have all written extensively on a variety of subjects in the art world, including several titles in the *Essential Art* series of books. They are currently living and working in or around London.

With thanks also to the Bridgeman Art Library, and especially Charlotte Kelly, for all her hard work in sourcing the images for this book. Grateful thanks to Helen Partington for her editorial assistance.

While every endeavour has been made to ensure the accuracy of the reproduction of the images in this book, we would be grateful to receive any comments or suggestions for inclusion in future reprints.

This is a Parragon Book
First published in 2000

Parragon
Queen Street House
4 Queen Street
Bath BA1 1HE, UK

Copyright © Parragon 2000

Created and produced for Parragon by
FOUNDRY DESIGN AND PRODUCTION,
a part of The Foundry Creative Media Co. Ltd
Crabtree Hall, Crabtree Lane
Fulham, London, SW6 6TY, UK

With special thanks to Josephine Cutts and Sasha Heseltine.
Jacket design by Kit Rocket for Parragon

ISBN: 0-75253-696-6

Printed and bound in Germany.

ESSENTIAL
History of
ART

$\boxed{p}$

Contents

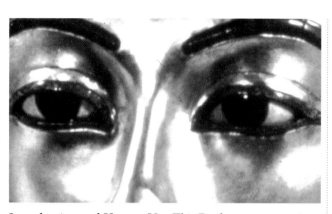

Introduction

ESSENTIAL History of Art introduces a new, chronological way of looking at the major movements in the Western art world over the last two thousand years. It is the only book to examine the roots of art in prehistory and provide seminal examples of work from 240 of the leading artists in the context of their school, period, vision and technique. For example, only in this book is it possible to compare a major work by Salvador Dalì to the work of contemporaries such as Pablo Picasso and René Magritte. Each artist is represented by a full-colour plate of an important work, and this is accompanied by text explaining their impact on and relevance to the development of art, and a brief history of the artist's life. Each entry is comprehensively cross-referenced and glossaries of artistic movements and technical terms are included at the end of the book. This book allows the reader to see the development of art chronologically within each specific movement, and in addition provides a source book for some of the most famous images in the Western world.

This date indicates the year in which the specific work of art was executed.

The name and life dates of the artist are given at the top of the page.

The featured work of art is presented in full colour.

The title of the featured work of art is given here.

The tab at the side of the page indicates which movement the artist belongs to and is colour-coded for ease of reference.

The text includes a brief history of the life of the artist and details the importance of this particular work of art.

Further works of art by the same artist are given in the yellow panel at the foot of the page.

Lascaux Cave Paintings

Galloping Horse
Caves of Lascaux, Dordogne, France. Courtesy of the Bridgeman Art Library

THE underground network of caves at Lascaux in the Dordogne, south-west France, contain Paleolithic wall paintings and engravings that depict animals, including horses, bison, cattle and deer. The civilisation that created these artworks lived in around 15,000 BC; it is probable that the caves were decorated as part of a magic ritual, perhaps to ensure a successful hunt.

The caves were rediscovered completely unintentionally in 1940 by a group of young boys who were out walking with a dog. The dog disappeared, and the caves were uncovered during the course of the search for the missing animal. The caves quickly attracted tourists from all over the world. In the mid-1960s the original cave site was closed to the public due to the rapid deterioration of the paintings caused by exposure to the atmosphere. Today visitors can see reproductions of the Paleolithic artworks in nearby caves.

The artworks vary enormously in size; some are larger than life size, others are small. The pigments used were natural earth colours mixed from dyes found in the local area. Some of the paintings and engravings are quite crudely sketched or etched outlines; others, such as the horse depicted here, have more detail, including well defined facial features and strong colouring.

Altamira Cave Paintings, Northern Spain, caves at the foot of Ayer's Rock (Uluru) in Australia, Dogon cliff paintings at Songo in Mali

ANCIENT ART

Palace of Minos, Knossos, Crete

Fresco of a Toreador
National Archaeological Museum, Athens. Courtesy of the Bridgeman Art Library

THE Minoan civilisation flourished from c.3000–1100 BC. The Palace of Minos at Knossos, in Crete, was one of three built by the early Minoans. It was ruined, along with the palaces of Phaistos and Mallia, when an earthquake devastated the entire area in c. 1700 BC. The palaces were rebuilt but another earthquake, in c. 1450 BC, destroyed them a second time. After the collapse of the Minoan civilisation at about the same time, the area was settled by the Mycenaeans.

The Palace of Minos was so named because it is believed to have been the home of the legendary King Minos, son of Zeus and Europa. In Greek mythology the palace also housed the labyrinth of the Minotaur – a creature with the head of a bull and the body

of a man, which required human flesh for sustenance. According to one story, the sea-god Poseidon took revenge on Minos for failing to sacrifice a white bull in his honour by causing his wife Pasiphaë to give birth to the Minotaur.

This fresco, which was excavated at the palace, appears to be of a bullfight – although no weapons are visible. The association with the Minotaur may explain the subject matter of the fresco.

 Fresco with Dolphins, Knossos, *Fowling Scene* from tomb of Nebamun, Thebes, *Revellers*, Tomb of the Leopards, Tarquinia

Egyptian Art

Death Mask of Tutankhamen

Egyptian National Museum, Cairo. Courtesy of the Bridgeman Art Library

ANCIENT Egypt has given the world some of its most spectacular art treasures, and this, the death mask of Tutankhamen, is perhaps the most famous. Throughout the 3,000 years of Pharaonic rule, there were 31 dynasties of ruling houses. Of these, Tutankhamen was only a relatively minor boy-king, who ruled for nine years during the era of the New Kingdom (1575–1087 BC).

The grave-goods of Tutankhamen have assumed enormous importance today because his tomb was found intact, whereas those of the greater pharaohs, such as Ramses II ('The Great'), who ruled for 67 years, were robbed many centuries ago. The treasures of Tutankhamen's grave included golden chariots, life-size statues, gems, precious metals, clothing and mummy cases. It is impossible to speculate on the wealth of treasure that was once contained in tombs of the more important pharaohs.

Created from gold and precious stones, including lapis lazuli, the death mask is breathtaking. The mask has symbolic significance: Tutankhamen's beard and headcloth (*nemes*) were symbols of his royalty; the cobra on his forehead was protective, its role being to spit poison at enemies of the pharaoh; lapis lazuli was also believed to have powers of protection.

Tomb of Ramses the Great, Relief of Akhenaten and his wife Nefertiti, Statue of Tuthmosis III

ANCIENT ART

Greek Sculpture

The Supplicant Barberini
Louvre, Paris. Courtesy of the Bridgeman Art Library

PORTRAIT sculpture was little known in Greece before the seventh century BC, when it became a recognisable, and respected, art form. The earliest Greek sculptures of people were evocative of the art of Ancient Egypt: there are many *kouros* (youths) and *kore* (young women) dating from around 650 BC which emulate Eyptian sculpture in their use of stylised eyes and static poses, and in their rigid portrayal of clothing.

However, Greek sculpture differed in one important respect – it was free-standing. Whereas Egyptian sculpture tended to remain fixed within a block of stone, in Greek sculpture any dispensable stone was cut away, creating space between the legs and between the arms and body; this technique allowed greater freedom of expression on the part of the sculptor and widened the range of subjects that were depicted.

The Supplicant Barberini dates from *c*. 400 BC. In comparison to the stiff, awkward *kouros* of an earlier era, it heralds an entirely new approach to marble portraiture. The face is far from stylised, depicting a real likeness, if not of Barberini then the face of the sculptor's model. The limbs are no longer static, and the drapery hangs in folds as real material would, in sharp contrast to the stiff, A-line robes of early *kore*.

Elgin Marbles, *Zeus and Ganymede, Hermes Carrying the Infant* *Dionysus*

CLASSICAL ART

Etruscan Art

Etruscan Amphora
Louvre, Paris. Courtesy of the Bridgeman Art Library

ETRUSCAN civilisation flourished in western Italy from *c.* 900 BC–*c.* 100 BC. Ancient Etruria encompassed modern Tuscany and parts of Umbria, and was roughly equivalent to the area between the rivers Arno and Tiber south of Florence, north of Rome and west of the Apennines.

Etruscan art was influenced by successive invasions of Asian, Greek and Roman civilisations. The technique of decorating pottery with 'red-figure painting' had been initiated in Etruria during the Greek period and remained in common practice during Roman times. Before this, the common decorative method had been 'black-figure painting', in which artists painted their work in black pigment on to a base of red clay. In Greek pottery, red-figure painting was a reversal of this, created by sketching the outline of the subject and then painting the background in black, leaving the design to show through in the colour of the clay. Etruscan artists, however, painted the entire surface of the clay in black and then painted over the top of this in a terracotta-coloured pigment.

The 'red-figure' pottery vase shown here probably dates from the early Roman occupation of Etruria, although it could be from the late-Greek era. It depicts a religious scene in honour of the god of wine, known as Bacchus to the Romans and Dionysus to the Greeks.

Tomb of the Bulls wall paintings, Tomb of the Sarcophagi sculptures, Tomb of the Painted Reliefs

Pompeiian Fresco

The Baker and His Wife
National Archaeological Museum, Naples. Courtesy of the Bridgeman Art Library

POMPEII was an ancient Roman country town near Naples in western Italy. It was destroyed, along with the neighbouring towns of Herculaneum and Stabiae, when Mount Vesuvius erupted in AD 79. Pompeii and its inhabitants were suffocated beneath the falling ash, although the town was perfectly preserved for centuries under successive layers of mud and vegetation.

In 1748 archaeologists began reclaiming Pompeii. The town appears to have been moderately wealthy and every house, from the most palatial to the most lowly, was decorated with wall paintings. Mosaics were also common.

Artwork found in Pompeii, Herculaneum and Stabiae is known as Campanian Art, and is representative of all southern Italian

painting at the time. As Pompeii was then under Roman rule it is also indicative of Roman art at this time, which had in turn been heavily influenced by earlier Greek art.

This particular work of art was painted on to a wall adjacent to the baker's house, and many believe that it depicts the baker, Paquius Proculus, and his wife. Others contend that the man, who has very dark, Latin features, may be a wealthy lawyer named Terentius Neus. The couple appear to be upper-class; the woman is elegantly dressed and coiffed, while he sports a white toga and carries a scroll.

 Theatre Scene, House of Augustus, Rome, fresco in House of Vetti, Pompeii, frescoes in Ipogeo degli Aureli, Rome

Basilica di San Marco, Venice

Bronze Horses (detail)
San Marco, Venice. Courtesy of the Bridgeman Art Library

THE four bronze horses now seen at the Basilica di San Marco in Venice were originally made for the Hippodrome in Constantinople (now Istanbul), which was then under Roman occupation. The Hippodrome could seat 60,000 spectators and was the largest in the ancient world. A low wall called a spina ran round much of the stadium and this was decorated with dozens of monuments, including the bronze horses. In 1204, during the crusades, the horses were stolen by Christian knights and taken to Venice.

For many years the four horses stood on the Loggia dei Cavalli (part of the basilica's façade), from where visitors can look out over St Mark's Square. Today the horses on the loggia are replicas; the originals were removed in 1979, in the cause of their preservation, and can now be seen inside the cathedral's museum. For centuries during medieval times these horses symbolised the power and prestige of the Venetian Republic; they were probably made during the 2nd century AD. It is not known whether their sculptor was Roman or Greek, although they are generally assumed to be Roman. The medium used was bronze, an alloy of copper and tin – the bronze used here was very rich in copper – and the bronze was then gilded.

 Antonia Minor, Museo Nazionale Romano, Rome, Statue of Marcus Aurelius, Piazza del Campidoglio, Rome, Gallienus, House of Vestal Virgins, Rome

CLASSICAL ART

Roman Catacombs

Aristotle with his Disciples

Catacomb della Via Latina, Rome. Courtesy of the Bridgeman Art Library

LYING outside the walls of the ancient city of Rome, these catacombs are probably the best preserved examples of early Christian art. The early converts to the religion decorated the resting-places of their dead in a similar manner to the Egyptians and Etruscans by painting frescoes directly on to walls built of untreated chalky subsoil, so it is remarkable that any of their delicate work has survived.

This fragile sepulchre art uses mostly simplistic colour and line, with solid figures placed in an illusionistic setting. To avoid possible confrontation with existing authorities, traditional classical and pagan motifs were adapted to express early Christian stories and concepts, although manipulation of the imagery was so subtle that it was only truly understood by cult members who had been initiated into the new church rituals.

This fresco, from a fresco cycle in the Catacomb della Via Latina, depicts the theme of salvation. The shift from pagan to early Christian imagery, further developed in later Byzantine art, can be seen in this image of Greek philosopher Aristotle with 12 disciples. Others in the cycle included Old Testament scenes of Daniel and the lions, Jonah and Noah, and New Testament tales of the loaves and fishes and the raising of Lazarus from the dead.

 Madonna and Child by Giotto, *The Last Judgement* by Cavallini, *David and Goliath*, Tahull, Spain

BYZANTINE

Mosaics from Ravenna

Christ Separates the Sheep from the Goats

Sant'Apollinare Nuovo, Ravenna. Courtesy of the Bridgeman Art Library

BYZANTINE art saw the fusion of pagan and Eastern iconography with early Christian images to create a highly influential artistic language of spiritual religiosity. The idealist philosophy of mystical knowledge – that man, through initiation, could transcend the world of appearances and gain admittance to the spiritual plane – saw images of reality transformed into esoteric symbols.

These stunning, Christian mosaics from Ravenna in Italy are among the earliest examples of the resplendent art produced by the Byzantine Empire between AD 330 and 1453. During the glorious 'Golden Ages' of Byzantine art – between the sixth and seventh centuries and from the ninth to the twelfth century – wall and panel paintings, illuminated manuscripts and mosaics were all subjected to the same lavish treatment, until realism of form returned with the early Renaissance and Humanist movement in the fifteenth century.

Byzantine art was concerned with symmetry and ornamentation rather than an imitation of life, reflecting the superior dimensions of an ideal universe. Images are seen suspended, as if in flight, against abstract gold backgrounds. Notions of horizon, expressive movement, and rational perspective, which had been explored by the Greeks in the half profile or three quarter view, were replaced with flat, full-frontal figures, as in this section of mosaic frieze from the church of Sant'Apollinare Nuovo.

 Justinian and Attendants, Procession of Martyrs, Three Kings

The Lindisfarne Gospels

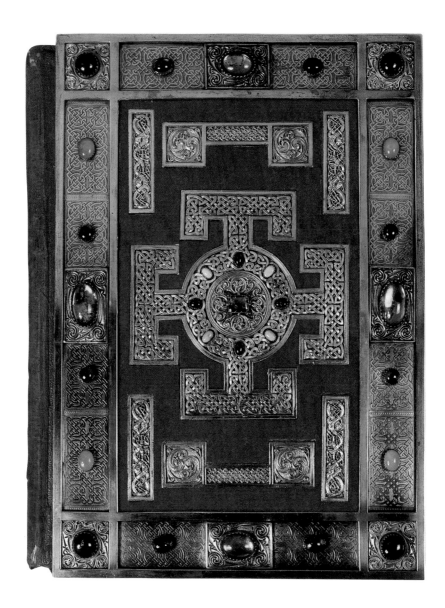

Front Cover Binding
Private Collection. Courtesy of the Bridgeman Art Library

IRISH missionary St Aidan (AD 600–651) arrived in Northumbria in AD 635 from the Scottish Hebridean island of Iona. He founded a monastery at Lindisfarne, where the *Lindisfarne Gospels* were created by Irish Monks. Their spectacular illuminations and jewel-encrusted binding reflect the importance of God's word, as spoken through the Bible.

According to notes added to the *Lindisfarne Gospels* in c. AD 950, the creator of the binding was a Bishop of Lindisfarne, Aethelwald. Another bishop, Eadfrith, was the scribe and, although it is not documented, he is also presumed to be the artist of the illuminated pictures. The translation of the text (from Latin into English) was undertaken by a priest of Lindisfarne, Aldred. In AD 875 Viking raids caused the monks to flee Lindisfarne, taking the gospels with them. They are now housed in the British Library, London.

This type of illumination is in the Hiberno-Saxon style, which encompasses elements of pagan art, such as Celtic design, as well as influences from elsewhere in Europe, including France and Germany. The Celtic element is apparent in the intricate design of the goldwork shown here. The use of gold and the many gems decorating the front cover are indicative of the wealth of the early Christian church.

Aelfric's *Anglo-Saxon Hexateuch*, *The Book of Durrow*, Aethelwald's *Benedictional*

The Apocalypse of Beatus

Martino and Petrus, Clericus

Capitular de Osma Archive, Soria. Courtesy of the Bridgeman Art Library

BEATUS was an Abbot who lived in Liébana, northern Spain. In *c.* AD 776 he wrote his masterpiece: a manuscript describing the *Apocalypse* – the biblical end of the world. The theme was a common one for scholars and religious leaders to write about. Beatus's Apocalypse was an extremely popular version of the story, which was reproduced by monastic communities for their own use. His work was passed down through generations of scholars and there are now 25 surviving copies, produced between the tenth and thirteenth centuries. These range in size from large-format manuscripts, obviously created for use in churches and cathedrals, to small illuminated manuscripts for personal use.

The version shown here was created in Beatus's native Spain, by monks who signed themselves 'Martino y Petrus, clericus'. The monks who painted illuminated manuscripts at this time were influenced by several artistic styles, most prominently Byzantine art, but also Celtic, Germanic and early Christian art. This version of Beatus's *Apocalypse* can still be seen in Soria, a province of central Spain, housed in the Archivo Capitular de Osma, in the village of El Burgo de Osma.

Gratian's *Decretum*, Helie de Borron's *Meliadus*, Bede's *Prose Life of St Cuthbert*

EARLY MEDIEVAL

The Book of Kells

Christy with Four Angels
Trinity College Library, Dublin. Courtesy of the Bridgeman Art Library

THE BOOK OF KELLS contains the four gospels in Latin, and was created by Irish monks living at Iona, an island in Scotland's Inner Hebrides. The pages are made of vellum and decorated with richly coloured dyes, some imported from the Middle East. Monks created such works as a sign of their obedience and devotion to God, believing that the word of God should only be recorded within scenes of beauty.

Iona was a place of great spirituality and learning, closely allied to Mayo Abbey in Ireland, another site of great religious import. St Columba, a sixth-century Irish missionary and priest, founded the monastery on Iona in *c.* AD 563, remaining there for the rest of his life. After his death (in AD 597), the monastery continued to thrive until the arrival of the first Viking marauders from Scandinavia in AD 804–07.

The Viking invasions caused the monks to flee to Kells in Ireland, leaving *The Book of Kells* unfinished. Nonetheless, it is one of the most spectacular surviving examples of illuminated medieval manuscripts, as the opening page of St Matthew's Gospel demonstrates. Today *The Book of Kells* is housed in the library of Trinity College, Dublin.

Bury Gospels, Oscott Psalter, Queen Melisande's Psalter

Harley Golden Gospels

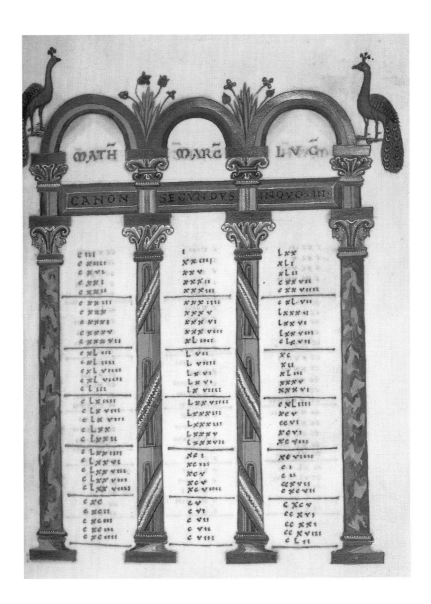

Canon Tables in Charlemagne's Court School

British Library. Courtesy of the Bridgeman Art Library

THE *Harley Golden Gospels* were created during the reign of Charlemagne (his birth date is unknown, but he became King of the Franks in AD 768 and died in AD 814). After Charlemagne was created Holy Roman Emperor, in AD 800, he attempted to improve the level of learning among his subjects, acquainting himself with many of the Western world's most learned scholars and ordering several manuscripts, including the *Harley Golden Gospels*, to be made. He created several royal workshops to produce the manuscripts; the *Harley Golden Gospels* were made at his workshop in Aachen in western Germany. At about the same time, Charlemagne ordered the creation of the Moutier Grandval Bible.

Despite their scholarly appeal, these works were commissioned not merely as an aid to learning, but also for their aesthetic qualities and their obvious monetary value. The Golden Gospels take their name from the fact that the script was produced in gold – an extremely expensive way of creating a manuscript. The manuscripts were great works of art that made a vital and valuable contribution to a monarch's status.

The Canon Tables showing the saints' days in Roman numerals are written in gold ink on to a *trompe-l'oeil*, giving the impression of a set of arches.

Moutier Grandval Bible, Bamberg *Apocalypse*, Utrecht Psalter

The Bayeux Tapestry

The Death of King Harold

Tapisserie Museum, Bayeaux. Courtesy of the Bridgeman Art Library

THE Bayeux Tapestry depicts events that happened in the years 1065–66, leading up to the Norman Conquest of England. It constitutes a vitally important historical record and is extremely valuable for the information it reveals about military tactics and equipment of the time. The scenes were embroidered, in two types of wool and eight different colours, on to a bare strip of linen and accompanied by a Latin text.

In fact, the Bayeux Tapestry is a fine example of medieval English embroidery, not a tapestry at all, and is thought to have been made in Canterbury, England. Tapestry is a medium in which the pattern is an integral part of the cloth, incorporated into the material as it is woven.

The story of William the Conqueror's defeat of the English King Harold in 1066 is depicted in 79 scenes, which span over 70 m (230 ft) in length and 50 cm (19.5 in) in height, and was probably commissioned by William's half-brother, Bishop Odo of Bayeux.

For many centuries the Bayeux Tapestry was apparently forgotten. It was not until the eighteenth century that it was rediscovered, by two French archaeologists. It is now on display in Bayeux, Normandy.

 Attainment, the Vision of the Holy Grail by Edward Burne-Jones and John Henry Dearle, *Scenes of the Trojan War* at Tournai, *The Months* series produced at the Gobelin workshops, Paris

Pietro Cavallini (c. 1250–c. 1330)

The Last Judgement (detail)
Santa Cecilia in Trastevere, Rome. Courtesy of the Bridgeman Art Library

PIETRO CAVALLINI was an Italian fresco painter and designer of mosaics, who spent most of his life in Rome. His dates of birth and death are unclear but he is known to have been artistically active between 1273 and 1308.

Cavallini was remarkable for his radical move away from the accepted Byzantine style of art. Although his work retained certain Byzantine elements, he also looked to other styles of art, in particular to the art of antiquity as well as more natural European influences. As a result, his work is imbued with a simplicity (although not to its detriment) unusual for its era.

Little of his work survives but his impressive fresco technique can be seen in *The Last Judgement*, which was painted for the church of Santa Cecilia in Trastevere in Rome. His move away from the Byzantine style is apparent in the pale colours he employed. His work is also notable for the individuality of the faces personifying Christ and his Apostles, painted to reflect each man's character and not to an archetypal ideal. A series of Cavallini's mosaics chronicling *The Life of the Virgin* (1291) can still be seen in Santa Maria in Trastevere, also in Rome.

 Life of the Virgin, Presentation in the Temple (detail from *Life of the Virgin*), *Life of St Francis*

Cimabue (c. 1240–1302)

Santa Trinità Madonna

Uffizi Gallery, Florence. Courtesy of the Bridgeman Art Library

CENNI DI PEPPI, known as Cimabue is traditionally believed to have been Giotto's (1267–1337) teacher and is credited with preparing the ground for the naturalism of Giotto's revolutionary style. By comparison with the latter's work, Cimabue's painting is flat and decorative, in keeping with the traditional Byzantine style, although it exhibited a naturalism and intensity that was unusual at the time. Cimabue's style may have sprung out of a visit he made to Rome in 1272, where mural painters and mosaicists were beginning to show an interest in creating naturalistic effects.

This image shows a traditional theme, in which the Virgin is enthroned with Christ in her arms and surrounded by angels. The painting is acknowledged as Cimabue's masterpiece and was originally executed for the altar at Santa Trinità in Florence. The Madonna and Child shows a sweetness and dignity that is unusual in Byzantine painting.

The faces of the angels, although similar, are expressive and seem to show an awareness of one another. Moreover, although Cimabue 'stacks' the angels on either side of the throne, with no real suggestion of depth, his architectural treatment of the throne shows an attempt to create a realistic, three-dimensional space – a new concept in art that was to be taken up with even greater effect by Giotto.

 St John, Madonna and Child, The Crucifix

The Kiss of Judas (detail)

Scrovegni (Arena) Chapel, Padua. Courtesy of the Bridgeman Art Library

THE Florentine painter Giotto is one of the most important artists in the history of Western art. A friend of the Italian poet Dante Alighieri (1265–1321) and reputed to be a pupil of Cimabue, he was the first artist of the medieval period to approach the human figure as a sculptural mass inhabiting its own space. He was also responsible for breaking with the saccharine sweetness found in the work of many earlier medieval artists. His work displays a complex language of communication, and for the first time portrays the real emotions of its subjects. When Giotto died in 1337, there was no one to take up his mantle of greatness. It was not until Masaccio (1401–c. 1428) that a suitable successor to his talents, innovation and skill appeared.

The fresco of *The Kiss of Judas* is a typical example of Giotto's portrayal of an emotionally intense encounter. The detail shows Judas about to kiss Jesus in the act of betrayal that will lead to his death. The gaze between the two is intense – it is obvious that Jesus knows what Judas is doing as he is betrayed. The fresco is part of Giotto's decoration, showing the lives of Christ and the Virgin, for the Arena Chapel in Padua.

La Navicella, Arena Chapel, Padua, *Ognissanti Madonna Crucifix* in Santa Maria Novella, Florence, Bardi Chapel in Santa Croce, Florence

GOTHIC MEDIEVAL

Maestà

Opera del Duomo Museum, Siena. Courtesy of the Bridgeman Art Library

DUCCIO, a near-contemporary of Cimabue, hailed from Siena, a city that had a great cultural rivalry with its close neighbour Florence, although the towns followed different artistic paths. As Italian art moved away from the Byzantine style of the Middle Ages, the Sienese school turned towards a decorative, almost courtly art, based on Byzantine traditions but marked by its use of colour and attention to detail.

In his early work Duccio was very close to Cimabue in style, with a concentration on pattern and very little attempt at depth. His influence, however, was more far-reaching than that of Cimabue, affecting the next two hundred years of Sienese painting. The *Maestà* (meaning 'majesty'), commissioned in 1308, was

installed in Siena Cathedral in 1311, and marked the culmination of Duccio's success. It was one of the largest panel paintings ever made in Italy. The central panel portrays the Madonna, child and saints. Around them and on the back are smaller scenes showing dramatic narratives from the life of Christ. In the painting Duccio shows a greater degree of naturalism than his contemporaries, especially in the formation of the drapery, and a new concern for space and perspective, although the figures are delicate and the traditional gold background serves to flatten the space.

Rucellai Madonna, Virgin Surrounded by St Peter, St Paul, St Augustine and St Dominic, London triptych

Andrea Pisano (c. 1290–1348)

John Baptises the People

The Baptistry Doors, Florence. Courtesy of the Bridgeman Art Library

ANDREA PISANO was born near Pisa. According to art historian Vasari (1511–74), he went to Florence to work on the west façade of the Duomo, which was designed by his friend Giotto. In 1330 he received a further commission to make a pair of bronze doors for the Baptistry in Florence. Pisano originally designed the East Doors but these were later moved to the south entrance to make way for Ghiberti's 'Gates of Paradise' (1425–59).

The doors were hung in 1336, and in 1340, three years after Giotto's death, Pisano became architect of the Duomo. In 1347 he was appointed Master of Works at Orvieto Cathedral.

Pisano's theme for the design of the Baptistry doors was the life of St John the Baptist. Set in a quatrefoil pierced by a square – a

French decorative motif – 20 bronze relief panels run across both doors, from left to right, telling the story of John's birth, ministry and death. Pisano's style – with sculpted, three-dimensional figures and an overall design aimed at creating drama – is profoundly influenced by that of Giotto. In panel nine, shown, the eye is drawn towards the figure of St John baptising the supplicant in the centre of the relief.

Reliefs on the lower register of the belltower of the Duomo in Florence, pulpit in Pisa Cathedral, pulpits in Sant' Andrea, Pistoia

GOTHIC MEDIEVAL

Ambrogio Lorenzetti (c. 1313–1348)

The Effects of Good Government

Palazzo Pubblico, Siena. Courtesy of the Bridgeman Art Library

AMBROGIO LORENZETTI was a Sienese painter and the younger brother of the artist Pietro (c. 1280–1348), who may have been his teacher. He was familiar with the work of Duccio and Simone Martini (c. 1284–1344), but his style owes much to the realism of Giotto (1267–1337). Lorenzetti painted rounded figures and showed a regard for space and depth, although the scale of the background in his work was not always accurate. However, until the early fourteenth century when architect Filippo Brunelleschi (1377–1446) worked out the mathematical rules of perspective, pictures were composed by eye alone.

The pair of frescoes showing *The Allegory of Good and Bad Government* were commissioned as a piece of civic propaganda for the *Sala dei Nove* in the Palazzo Pubblico, Siena. Both works were extraordinary at the time for showing a contemporary panorama of a real place with real people.

The Effects of Good Government shows Siena as a place of peace and prosperity, with evidence of commerce, active building, agriculture and industry. Although the frescoes are not dated with certainty, they belong to Lorenzetti's mature work. After 1348 there are no further records of either brother being active and it is thought that they died from the Black Death, which struck Europe that year.

 The Charity of St Nicholas Bari, The Presentation in the Temple, The Annunciation

Jean, Paul and Herman Limbourg

January from *Les Très Riches Heures du Duc de Berry*

The Victoria and Albert Museum, London. Courtesy of the Bridgeman Art Library

THE artistic partnership of the three Limbourg brothers created this celebrated illuminated prayer book, one of several known as 'books of hours'; the 'hours' were in the form of prayers to be recited at set times throughout the day. The exquisite depictions of courtly love and chivalric imagery contain powerful iconography which has endured throughout the centuries and influenced much subsequent work.

The Limbourg brothers, who were born in Flanders but worked in France, gained international acceptance for their highly desirable Flemish style, which was well expressed in manuscript form. The style was renowned for its rich, bright colours and reproductions of landscape directly from nature, a pioneering approach that was to have a profound effect on French art and led to the evolution of realism later in the fifteenth century.

Les Très Riches Heures was commissioned by the Duke of Berry, an influential patron of the arts – he was one of the era's most important art collectors and brother of the powerful Duke of Burgundy (Philip the Good, 1419–67). The duke was well known for his raids on Europe and the East for art treasures. The month of 'January', seen here, with its carnival of colour and highly decorative detail, shows the duke probably returning from such a raiding foray to a sumptuous court banquet held in his honour.

 Limbourg's *Belles Heures*, *Bible Moralisé*, Froissart's *Chronicles*

Gentile da Fabriano (c. 1370–1427)

The Presentation of the Child in the Temple
Louvre, Paris. Courtesy of the Bridgeman Art Library

GENTILE DA FABRIANO's work is a stunning example of the blending of International Gothic style with the early Renaissance works of fifteenth-century Florence. During this period the Lombardy and Venetian regions of Italy were artistically closer to the development in oils associated with the Flanders' workshops than to nearby Florence.

Da Fabriano produced memorable images of the medieval mind: an adoration of nature. His fascination with detail and vignettes of jewellery, birds and dogs are similar to Giotto's earlier creations but without the concentration on monumental figures. He created a vibrant effect, seen in the intricately worked picture shown here and his other celebrated masterpiece, *Adoration of the Magi* (1423).

The effects of Humanist philosophy on the fourteenth century broke art's bondage to theology, allowing some acknowledgement of the 'real' secular world. Instead of adherence to the Florentines' rational, geometric approach, the International Gothic movement allowed intuition to take the lead. The representational lyricism of *The Presentation of the Child in the Temple* reflects this move, although medieval problems concerning space and depth are still an issue. Here, notions of perspective are accomplished through strong bands of horizontal line, the use of a central light source in the main tableau and the angular forms of the buildings.

 Adoration of the Magi, Madonna and Child, Crowning the Virgin

Robert Campin (c. 1375–1444)

Virgin and Child Before a Firescreen

Hermitage, St Petersburg. Courtesy of the Bridgeman Art Library

KNOWN as the Master of Flémalle, Campin, alongside Jan van Eyck (1390–1441), was one of the most influential masters of the early Flemish school. Working at Tournai in Flanders, he was one of the first artists to experiment with the reintroduction of oil-based colours, instead of painting with egg-based tempera, to achieve the brilliance of colour typical with this period.

Campin used the new technique to convey strong, rounded characters by modelling light and shade in compositions of complex perspectives. A pioneer of new facial types and characteristics, Campin was the first artist to try to capture and portray in his painting the sitter's personality. He was also bold in experimenting with traditional religious imagery, creating a cosy Flanders home setting for his *Merode Annunciation* triptych (1428), instead of the traditional gold backdrop. Subsequently, his workshop had influence throughout European art during the fifteenth century.

Here, in a similar ground-breaking domestic setting for the Virgin and child, the emphasis is on solid, monumental forms and the effects of light falling on the rich folds of the Virgin's dress. Campin has succeeded in subverting a deeply revered image of religious iconography into a blissful moment of relaxed intimacy between mother and child; this is the Son of God portrayed as a human baby, with very real demands for maternal attention.

 Joseph in his Workshop, Nativity, Portrait of a Woman

The Arnolfini Marriage

The National Gallery, London. Courtesy of the Bridgeman Art Library

THE early Flemish school's greatest artist, Jan van Eyck, along with his contemporary, Rogier van der Weyden (1399–1464), was responsible for the spread of the International Gothic style. He worked for the French Duke of Burgundy, acted as court envoy to Spain and Portugal and as diplomat and city official in Bruges from 1430. Some believe he invented oil painting because of his advanced use of the medium. In fact, this technique had been known since antiquity, but Van Eyck used it as never before to portray sensational lighting effects of great clarity and realism.

His skilful development of oil's translucent properties is explored on a variety of textures in this landmark double portrait, one of the greatest pictures of the second millennium. It was probably a bourgeois commission to commemorate the couple's betrothal; as

such, it is one of the very first genre paintings, in a style that depicts the lives of ordinary people rather than concentrating on the sole portrayal of religious subjects.

Although ignorant of one-point perspective, Van Eyck achieves visual balance through a subtly lit interior and compositional symmetry, with the medial line of the perfectly centralised mirror falling between the betrothed couple. Whether the reflection in the mirror is of the priest or Van Eyck himself is regularly debated.

Man in a Red Turban, Madonna with Canon van der Paele, Madonna with Chancellor Rolin

Antonio Pisanello (c. 1395–1455)

Lionel d'Este
Accademia Carrara Gallery, Bergamo. Courtesy of the Bridgeman Art Library

THE successor to Gentile da Fabriano, Pisanello worked in Verona. Like his master, he was fascinated with the bejewelled tapestry effects that could be created using the new oil medium that had been pioneered by the Flanders workshops. The medium suited the climate of Italy much better than the cold, damp Low Countries of northern Europe. Pisanello painted frescoes at Verona in Italy, where two survive, and also in Venice and Rome, though these have since been destroyed.

Pisanello's work is characterised by naturalism and a detailed observation of reality. The spectacular *Vision of St Eustace* is a wonderfully vibrant perception of enchantment and a splendid example of Pisanello's subtle synthesis of fact and fantasy. Despite the obvious influence of the International Gothic style, he shared the Florentine preoccupation with structure, foreshortening and one-point perspective in his draughtsmanship.

The most renowned court painter and medallist of his time, Pisanello was a draughtsman of genius: his drawings became models for the later Renaissance artists. This portrait of Lionel d'Este, a member of one of Verona's chief families and a patron of the arts, reveals his wonderful manipulation of oil and his subtle introduction of light.

St George and the Princess, Vision of St Eustace, The Virgin and Child with St George and St Anthony Abbot

INTERNATIONAL GOTHIC

Rogier van der Weyden (1399–1464)

Portrait of a Lady
The National Gallery, London. Courtesy of the Bridgeman Art Library

AFTER Jan van Eyck, Rogier van der Weyden was the most influential Flemish artist of the fifteenth century. He travelled widely throughout Europe, always encouraging the adoption of revolutionary new oil techniques to achieve effects of realism and natural light. No signed paintings have survived and little is known about Van der Weyden's life except that he was probably apprenticed to Roger Campin, the Master of Flémalle, whose workshop dominated the artistic century.

Van der Weyden lived in Brussels and became the city's official painter in 1436. He travelled to Italy in 1450, influencing painting there and absorbing the Italian trend for a warm, bright palette. Like the Limbourg brothers before him, he was commissioned by the Duke of Burgundy to paint court portraits, spreading his artistic authority into France.

His lighting had a profound impact on religious art, bathing the subject's symbolic detail in an other-worldly atmosphere. Warmer in palette than Van Eyck, he was less concerned with the realistic representation of space, concentrating on the significance of action and his sitter's emotions, seen here in *Portrait of a Lady*. His work pioneered the projection of mood and emotion in painting that was highly influential on the development of art.

 Deposition, Last Judgement, Portrait of Antione de Bourgogne

Benozzo Gozzoli (c. 1421–97)

The Journey of the Magi (detail)
Palazzo Medici-Riccardi, Florence. Courtesy of the Bridgeman Art Library

THE Florentine painter Gozzoli took over the poetic mantle of Gentile da Fabriano in producing richly tapestried landscapes of immense beauty and colour. In his youth he was an assistant to Lorenzo Ghiberti (1378–1455), working on the Baptistry doors in Florence. He also assisted Fra Angelico (*c.* 1387–1455) with frescoes in the Vatican, but later gained a reputation as a painter in his own right, going on to paint frescoes and altarpieces in a number of towns including Rome, San Gimignano and Pisa.

The International Gothic style synthesised the decorative elements of the Flemish school with the realism of Italian art, and in Gozzoli's painting we can see a renewed sensitivity to landscape settings, a progression in the use of new facial types and further attempt at the portrayal of psychological characteristics in the individuals depicted in the paintings.

In *The Journey of the Magi*, Gozzoli shows an awareness of depth and spatial values. Bands of colour are broken up by the structural element of the zigzagging road that runs up the centre of the picture line to create a sensation of distance and horizon, as well as movement. Gozzoli's most famous fresco, it was painted in the small chapel of the Palazzo Medici-Riccardi in Florence, during the hot summer of 1459, which explains the brilliance of the gold and azure lighting effects, reminiscent of Gentile da Fabriano's work.

🖌 *Madonna and Child with Saints, Life of St Augustine, Angels*

Dieric Bouts (c. 1415–75)

Virgin and Child
Private Collection. Courtesy of the Bridgeman Art Library

BELIEVED to be a pupil of Rogier van der Weyden, Bouts shared his master's love of rich colour and realism, exploring their effects on spatial relationships, perspective and composition. A native of Haarlem, he moved to Louvain in the more prosperous south of the Low Countries, which brought him closer to Brussels and the great studios of Van Eyck and Van der Weyden. Under their influence, his distinctive style gained maturity and control, enabling him to express a deep spiritual beauty through a portrayal of detached stillness similar to Van Eyck's. He became Louvain's civic painter in 1468, and one of his commissions was the *Last Supper* triptych, which he painted in the last years of his life.

In common with other Flemish artists, Bouts worked on highly polished wood panels, using oils mixed with colour pigments to achieve a transparent finish and brilliant colour. The fine details seen in his work, which were executed with minute brushstrokes, reveal his mastery of his medium, as shown in this tender work.

The Virgin's face is rendered with an acute level of psychological understanding, and is expressive of the tenderness she feels for Christ, just as any mother would feel for her son. Bouts achieves a sense of tranquillity in the work by surrounding the mother and baby with a shimmering gold light.

Justice of the Emperor Otto, The Last Supper triptych, Paradise of the Symbolic Fountain

Hans Memling (c. 1433–94)

The Mystic Marriage of St Catherine
Louvre, Paris. Courtesy of the Bridgeman Art Library

BORN near Frankfurt, Hans Memling was a pupil of the highly influential Flemish master, Rogier van der Weyden, and worked mainly in Bruges, Flanders, in an atmosphere that became increasingly conservative as the century progressed. Memling's work has been criticised as insipid and conventional, but his sensitive portrait work is highly accomplished. His paintings influenced artists beyond Flanders, although they are overshadowed by the work of his master, Van der Weyden. However, Memling's quiet, contemplative style was highly successful in his day – he owned four houses and was included on a list of Bruges' richest citizens.

This composition, which forms part of a triptych, was painted for the Hôpital de St Jean in Bruges, where it remains today in a museum of the artist's work. The two other side panels depict complex images: *Beheading the Baptist* and *The Vision of St John the Evangelist on Patmos*.

Using a technique developed by Van der Weyden, Memling paints the folded flowing drapery of the two seated female saints, St Catherine and St Barbara, in a way that injects energy into an otherwise static, stolidly composed scene. Memling developed this technique in a later work, *The Shrine of St Ursula* (1489), which had a narrative style that impacted on early Renaissance Italian artists such as Vittore Carpaccio (c. 1455–1525).

 Man with an Arrow, The Shrine of St Ursula, The Deposition

Hieronymous Bosch (c. 1450–1516)

The Garden of Earthly Delights
Prado, Madrid. Courtesy of the Bridgeman Art Library

ONE of the last of the great medieval Flemish painters, Netherlandish painter Bosch explored a highly imaginative world of religious symbolism and allegory, from horrific images of hell through to visions of heavenly delight.

Weird, colourful and playful, he ignored the influences of the early Italian Renaissance, which were beginning to spread across the cultural divides of Europe. Bosch's sense of colour and form seems strikingly modern, and analogies have been drawn between his work and that of the twentieth century's Expressionist and Surrealist movements. Little is known about his life, except that he was born at Hertogenbosch, in the south of the Netherlands, and his father was a wood craftsman. Although he knew the

pioneering realism of the works of Flemish painters such as Jan van Eyck and Robert Campin, he developed his own fantastical style, with depictions of distorted creatures reminiscent of classical 'grotesque' imagery – chaotic mural decorations of flora and fauna. He was very popular in his lifetime; his works were often forged.

In the stunning triptych for *The Garden of Earthly Delights*, each panel is endowed with its own meaning. The landscape is minutely detailed, brightly coloured and freakish, complemented by bizarre imaginary creatures and figures. A fourth painting, *The Third Day of Creation*, is revealed when the triptych is closed.

 The Tribulations of St Anthony, The Adoration, Last Judgement

Matthias Grünewald (c. 1475–1528)

The Crucifixion

Staatliche Kunsthalle, Karlsruhe. Courtesy of the Bridgeman Art Library

THE graphic horror and emotional intensity portrayed by artists of the International Gothic movement is felt particularly in the work of German artist, Matthias Grünewald. As a contemporary of Albrecht Dürer (1471–1528) and a court painter, his art verges on the macabre, with dark, sombre imagery and themes.

He is renowned for a series of ten paintings undertaken for the cathedral altar in Isenheim, Alsace. They were intended to be seen in three groups, which changed as the altar panels were alternately opened and closed; the image of *The Crucifixion* appeared next to *St Anthony and St Sebastian*. The undercurrent of violence is acute in this section, as the mutilated body of Christ expires in agony on the oversized cross, which bends with the weight of his slumped torso. The hands are distorted in the final moment of anguish. The faithful mourners grouped below the cross are oddly set against the exaggerated form of Christ. All this is placed in the dark setting of a wasteland, quite unlike the glowing tapestry of colour used by early exponents of the International Gothic style such as Gentile da Fabriano. Yet it is the very freedom of expression inherent in the ideals of the International Gothic movement that allowed the creative impetus necessary for the portrayal of such naked, anguished emotion.

St Anthony and St Paul, The Mocking of Christ, The Virgin at the Entombment

c. 1427 Masaccio (Tommaso di Giovanni) (1401–28)

The Expulsion of Adam and Eve from Paradise

Brancacci Chapel, Santa Maria del Carmine, Florence. Courtesy of the Bridgeman Art Library

DOCUMENTARY evidence of Masaccio was first recorded in 1422, when he entered the Florentine Guild of Artists. In his short life – he died at the age of 27, possibly from malaria – he produced enough work for later artists to hail him as the successor to Giotto and the precursor of Michelangelo (1475–1564).

At a time when the Gothic style was flourishing, Masaccio, with his friends Donatello (1386–1466) and Filippo Brunelleschi (1377–1446), introduced a dramatic, heroic style in which realism and form were superior to the decorative effects of line.

Masaccio's genius is exemplified in his solid, weighty realism and gift for rendering pictorial space in perspective. He had a profound understanding of classical art and an aptitude for narrative that reveals itself in the psychology of his figures – their gestures and expressive faces – as well as in the interactive quality of his compositions. Even his backgrounds contribute to the mood and narrative flow.

In this fresco, Masaccio uses a downward, left-to-right diagonal to emphasise the fall of Adam and Eve from grace – an effect which is enhanced by the fact that we look up at the fresco. Masaccio's other important frescoes, including *The Tribute Money* and *The Expulsion*, can also be seen in the Brancacci Chapel in Santa Maria del Carmine, Florence.

 Virgin and Child, The Expulsion, The Tribute Money

Masolino (da Panicale) (c. 1383–1447)

St Peter Raising a Cripple and the Resurrection of Tabitha

Brancacci Chapel, Santa Maria del Carmine, Florence. Courtesy of the Bridgeman Art Library

THE first known reference to Masolino occurs in 1423, when he was accepted into the Florentine Guild of Artists, which allowed him to employ assistants in his studio. It is thought that he worked on Lorenzo Ghiberti's first set of Baptistry doors.

Highly regarded in his own time, he has since constantly been compared with Masaccio, who collaborated with him on several works, most importantly the decoration of the Brancacci Chapel in Santa Maria delle Carmine, Florence.

In 1426 Masolino went to Hungary with *condottiere* (mercenary) Pippo Spano for two years, leaving Masaccio to continue work on the chapel. Thereafter, Masolino reverted to the International Gothic style, which was still popular in Florence. He travelled to Rome, working in San Clemente, and in 1435 is known to have been working in Castiglione d'Olona near Milan.

Naturally a Gothic artist, with a delicate, decorative style, Masolino's work in the Brancacci Chapel does show Masaccio's influence, although their differences in style are marked. This fresco shows two episodes linked by a pair of foppish, typically sweet-faced young messengers, dressed in flat, rich brocades and showing little urgency for their mission. Significantly, the haloes of St Peter and St John disobey the rules of perspective.

 Madonna and Child, The Crucifixion, Baptism of Christ

Lorenzo Ghiberti (1378–1455)

Joseph Sold into Slavery

The Baptistry, Florence. Courtesy of the Bridgeman Art Library

LORENZO GHIBERTI, a Florentine goldsmith and sculptor, rose to prominence in 1401 when he won the commission to make one of the two remaining sets of bronze, gilded doors for the Baptistry, beating both sculptor and architect Filippo Brunelleschi and the Sienese sculptor Jacopo della Quercia (1374–1438).

Ghiberti completed the North Doors before working on the East Doors (1425–59), using Donatello's technique of flattened relief. Taking ten Old Testament stories, he created ten panels showing various episodes within masterly compositions of perspective – a contrast to his earlier doors, in which the figures exist as three-dimensional miniatures on a single plane. The panel shown includes four episodes in the story of Joseph.

The doors were so highly esteemed that they were placed on the east side of the Baptistry, replacing Pisano's earlier creations, where they became a great source of inspiration to other artists. Ghiberti was prominent in the artistic revival of Florence and his large workshop produced several artists of great stature, including Donatello, Masolino and Paolo Uccello (c. 1397–1475). Ghiberti also designed goldsmith's work, reliquaries, stained-glass windows for Florence Cathedral, and wrote prolifically, leaving the first surviving autobiography of an artist.

 Sacrifice of Isaac, St John the Baptist, Reliquary of St Zenobius

Fra Angelico
(Guido di Pietro) (c. 1387–1455)

The Annunciation
San Marco dell'Angelico Museum, Florence. Courtesy of the Bridgeman Art Library

FRA ANGELICO'S early career is obscure. He did not take up painting until 1417 and, although his early work was in the International Gothic style, he continued the innovations in perspective introduced by Masaccio.

As a Dominican monk within a teaching order, Fra Angelico's work served a didactic rather than a purely mystical purpose. His style is correspondingly simple, while his contemporaries, such as Masolino, were experimenting with a Neo-Gothic style. Like Fra Filippo Lippi (1406–69), he painted early examples of the *sacra conversazione* (sacred conversation).

In 1438, he and his assistants began painting a series of 50 frescoes to decorate the monks' cells at the monastery of San Marco in Florence. *The Annunciation* is one of these. The frescoes were created as aids to prayer and contemplation; their straightforward composition, limited colour and lack of superfluous detail give them a humble grandeur and serenity. Although Fra Angelico uses the realism and perspectival techniques learned from Masaccio, his halos and wings are flat, painted in the Gothic style.

Fra Angelico was later commissioned to work at the Vatican, where his frescoes are more ornate, with an emphasis on narrative and detail that was deemed more appropriate for a public palace.

The Linaiuoli Madonna, Madonna and Saints, Lives of St Stephen and St Lawrence

c. 1440 Donatello (Donato di Niccolo) (1386–1466)

David
Bargello, Florence. Courtesy of the Bridgeman Art Library

A SCULPTOR in marble and bronze, Donatello was the most influential and innovative artist of the early Quattrocento. With his friend Masaccio, and the architects Leon Battista Alberti (1404–72) and Filippo Brunelleschi (1377–1440), he created the monumental realism that was the defining quality of the early Renaissance in Florence.

Trained in Lorenzo Ghiberti's studio, his early commissions included the decorations for the church of Orsanmichele, for which he created vast, freestanding niche statues. Despite the prevailing popularity of the International Gothic style, Donatello created figures of strength and psychological tension, disregarding the surface finish of a sculpture in order to achieve the correct visual effects of light and shade. He was well-known for distorting the proportions of his figures. In 1417 Donatello introduced the technique of *rilievo schiacciato* or 'flattened relief', as shown in the base relief of his St George in Orsanmichele. This inspired Ghiberti's East Doors (*c.* 1435) for the Baptistry in Florence.

The elongated and effeminate bronze figure of *David* was influenced by a classical concern for anatomy and is thought to be the first nude, freestanding figure made since classical antiquity. In his later years, Donatello experimented with form and content to achieve work of disturbing intensity.

 Judith and Holofernes, San Rossore, Crucifix

Fra Filippo Lippi (c. 1406–69)

The Annunciation

San Lorenzo, Florence. Courtesy of the Bridgeman Art Library

AN ORPHAN, Filippo Lippi grew up in the monastery of the Carmine in Florence, taking holy orders – for which he was unsuited – in 1421. His talent was apparent at an early age and he copied from Masaccio's ground-breaking frescoes in the Brancacci Chapel. Lippi's major achievement is the fresco cycle (1452–66) in the cathedral at Prato. During his time in Prato he was tortured, put on trial for fraud and had an affair with a nun, Lucrezia Buti. Lippi was rescued on each occasion by his patron, Cosimo de' Medici il Vecchio (1389–1464).

Lippi's Barbadori altarpiece (1437) in Santo Spirito, Florence, is one of the first datable examples of the *sacra conversazione* (sacred conversation), in which the Virgin, Child and saints inhabit the same space – a format that superseded the Virgin and Child enthroned in majesty with saints arranged in panels on either side.

Lippi's work shows the profound influence of both Masaccio and Donatello, but he replaces the chiaroscuro, solidity and prescribed space of Masaccio with a sweeter, linear style reminiscent of the Gothic style. The altarpiece also shows the influence of Flemish art, which is most noticeable in the translucent vase in the foreground. Lippi's later religious works, especially the *Nativities*, are increasingly imbued with religious feeling.

The Tarquinia Madonna, Madonna and Child, Madonna Adoring her Child

Andrea Mantegna (1431–1506)

The Agony in the Garden
The National Gallery, London. Courtesy of the Bridgeman Art Library

PUPIL and adopted son of Francesco Squarcione (1397–c. 1468), Mantegna grew up in Padua, and was surrounded by humanist ideas, classical nude studies and the sculptures of Donatello, all of which influenced his style. His paintings were marked by a passion for classical architecture and a profound mastery of perspective and foreshortening – qualities evident by 1448 when he began a series of frescoes for the Ovetari Chapel in Eremetani Church, Padua, which was destroyed in 1944.

In 1460 Mantegna became court painter to Ludovico Gonzaga at Mantua – a town that rivalled the artistic centres of Rome and Florence. He decorated the Ducal Palace with frescoes glorifying the Gonzaga family. Most notably, he introduced the classical feature of painting illusory architecture that seemed to extend into a real perspective. The same technique was also used by Raphael (1483–1520) and Correggio (c. 1490–1534), but not fully exploited until the Baroque period in the seventeenth century.

The Agony in the Garden, based on a sketch by Jacopo Bellini (c. 1400–70), is an excellent example of Mantegna's sharp, analytical style. Other works, such as the *Crucifixion* (c. 1459), are notable for their innovative compositions. His experiments with viewpoints and the sculpted and tinted stone or bronze quality of his forms also illustrate the influence of Donatello.

 Parnassus, The Triumph of Caesar, The Dead Christ

Piero della Francesca (c. 1416–92)

Federigo da Montefeltro, Duke of Urbino
Uffizi Gallery, Florence. Courtesy of the Bridgeman Art Library

PIERO DELLA FRANCESCA's work is remarkable for its synthesis of mid-fifteenth-century Italian painting, with its deep interest in perspective and space, and Flemish painting, with all its study of light, bright colours and natural phenomena and detail. His work is dominated by a serene grandeur, and has very little sense of movement. Instead, it is based on the strict mathematical principles of geometry and perspective.

Moving from his home town of Borgo San Sepolcro to Florence, Piero was influenced by the work of Fra Angelico and Paolo Uccello, from whom he derived his solid figures, love of colour and fascination with perspective and space. He absorbed the influences of Flemish art, which was beginning to infiltrate Florentine culture

in the 1430s. After 1442 he worked in Ferrara, Rimini, Arezzo, Rome and Urbino. The frescoes at Arezzo (1452–c. 1459), which depict *The Story of the True Cross*, are among his most important works. The *Brera Madonna* (c. 1475), one of his last works, is an early *sacra conversazione* piece, with a use of perspective that seems to expand into the church.

The Flemish influences on Piero's work can be seen in this portrait of his patron, in the play of light, the details of hair and skin, the background landscape and the oil medium.

The Baptism of Christ, The Flagellation, Brera Madonna and Saints

Paolo Uccello (c. 1396–1475)

The Hunt in the Forest
Ashmolean Museum, Oxford. Courtesy of the Bridgeman Art Library

EARLY RENAISSANCE

UCCELLO was apprenticed to Lorenzo Ghiberti between 1407 and 1415, although he never worked as a sculptor. In 1425 he went to Venice to work as a mosaicist and returned to Florence by 1432, where he produced two frescoes depicting scenes from the Old Testament in the Green Cloister in Santa Maria Novella. These were organised across a single plane in which linear perspective was not used. His first dated work of 1436, a large fresco of the English mercenary Sir John Hawkwood, reveals his new-found fascination with perspective.

Uccello's work combines both the decorative, elaborate spirit of the International Gothic style, which he would have learned in Ghiberti's studio, with the new laws of early Renaissance perspective. He is often considered somewhat fanatical about the treatment of perspective in painting, although he did not always get it right. *The Deluge* (1445), also in the Green Cloister, shows the impact of the new ideas on perspective at their most powerful.

This painting, generally considered a late work and painted in oil on panel, combines Gothic and early Renaissance styles with a fairy-tale charm. Although in some ways the regularity of the design creates an almost medieval effect, the movement of the dogs and horses balances the composition with a darting energy.

 Sir John Hawkwood, The Battle of San Romano, St George and the Dragon

Antonio (c. 1432–98) and
Piero (1443–96) del Pollaiuolo

The Martyrdom of St Sebastian
The National Gallery, London. Courtesy of the Bridgeman Art Library

THE Pollaiuolo brothers were goldsmiths, engravers, sculptors, painters and designers of embroideries, and owned one of the most successful workshops in Florence during the second half of the fifteenth century. There are few known works by Piero – it appears that Antonio was largely responsible for most of the work of quality that emerged from their workshop.

The brothers' work is characterised by a fascination with the human body in motion. Their capacity to model realistic three-dimensional figures was based on a thorough understanding of human anatomy. The influences of Donatello, a key figure in Renaissance sculpture, and Andrea del Castagno (c. 1421–57), known for his powerful portrayal of figures, are paramount in their

work – in fact, Piero is thought to have been a pupil of Del Castagno for a short time.

The pyramidal composition of this painting is not based on any preconceived shape, but rooted in the actions of the archers. The archers are portrayed from every angle – in effect, there are only two poses – in an exploration of straining sinews and taut muscles. The background, showing the Flemish influence in its pioneering interest in landscape, is full of action. The figure of St Sebastian (possibly painted by Piero) is somewhat overshadowed by the movement surrounding him.

Labours of Hercules, Daphne and Apollo, Battle of the Nude Gods

EARLY RENAISSANCE

Antonello da Messina (c. 1430–79)

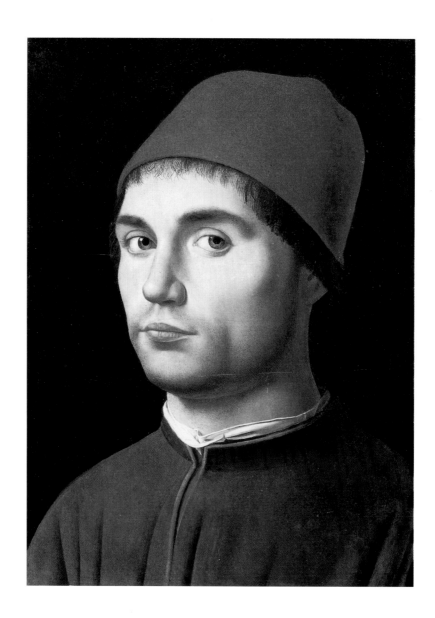

Portrait of a Young Man
The National Gallery, London. Courtesy of the Bridgeman Art Library

ANTONELLO DA MESSINA was a Sicilian and the only major fifteenth-century painter born south of Rome. He trained in Naples, where he was influenced by Flemish painting, particularly the work of Jan van Eyck. His first known work is a portrait of *Salvator Muni*, which he painted in 1465. In 1475–76 he visited Venice, where his work had a profound effect on the artistic community. His Flemish realism and attention to detail, when combined with the grandeur of Italian art, was revolutionary. He also popularised the use of oils – a technique widespread in northern Europe but then little used in Italy.

Da Messina's most influential work in Venice was the San Cassiano altarpiece, of which two fragments remain. In the *sacra conversazione*, the architectural setting of the painting extends by *trompe-l'oeil* into the chapel itself – the Madonna, Child and saints appear to inhabit the same space as the viewer.

Portrait of a Man reveals Da Messina's Flemish influences – in the three-quarter, rather than the side, view, the lively glance and the precise detail. The depiction of light, used to accentuate the clearly modelled features, was also a typical feature of northern European art. The dark background, another northern technique, focuses attention on the well-lit face.

 Ecce Homo, St Jerome in his Study, Polyptych in San Gregorio

Luca della Robbia (1400–82)

Madonna and Child (glazed terracotta relief)
The Victoria and Albert Museum, London. Courtesy of the Bridgeman Art Library

LUCA DELLA ROBBIA came from a family of artists, of whom he is the best known. Nothing is known of his early career but he was considered by the contemporary art theorist Leon Battista Alberti (1404–72) to be as important an innovator in the new Renaissance style as his contemporaries Donatello and Lorenzo Ghiberti. However, he is now chiefly remembered for the glazed terracotta plaquettes that he introduced as a sculptural medium. The studio of Della Robbia seems to have kept the terracotta formula a secret, enabling him to establish a flourishing business.

One of his most famous works, and the first documented of its type, is the *Cantoria* (1431–38), or singing gallery, in Florence Cathedral, which shows a cheerful rendition of cherub musicians reflecting antique prototypes. It is paired with a *cantoria* designed by the sculptor Donatello.

The plaquette shown here is one of several half-length, blue-and-white *Madonna and Child* terracotta reliefs which show that Della Robbia's major concern was to represent a three-dimensional shape on a flat plane. He also used yellow and green in his reliefs. The studio was taken over by Della Robbia's nephew Andrea (1435–1525), and thereafter by his sons, of whom the most important, artistically, was Giovanni della Robbia (1469–1529).

Roundels of the Apostles in the Pazzi Chapel, Santa Croce, *The Resurrection*, *The Ascension*, both in Florence Cathedral

Carlo Crivelli (c. 1435–95)

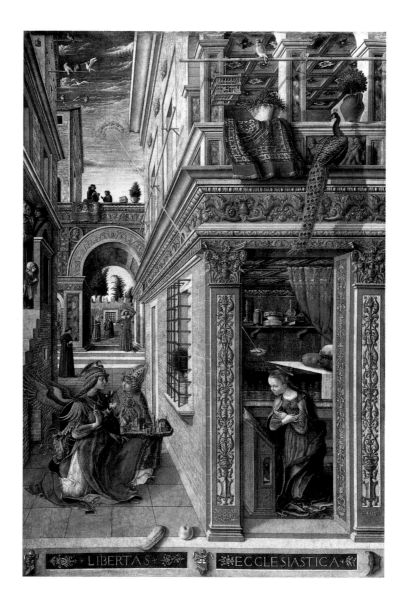

The Annunciation with St Emidius

The National Gallery, London. Courtesy of the Bridgeman Art Library

CARLO CRIVELLI was a Venetian and a contemporary of the Bellini brothers and Andrea Mantegna. In 1457 he was expelled from Venice for committing adultery, first working in Dalmatia (now Croatia) and then moving to the Italian Marches: he never returned to Venice after this, but always persisted in signing himself as a Venetian.

As a result, Crivelli worked in an artistic vacuum, away from the great Renaissance centres of Florence, Venice and Rome. Before his expulsion he may have worked in the Vivarini workshop in Venice. He may have had some experience in Padua, where it is possible that he absorbed influences from Mantegna – his work has the same attention to detail and interest in classical archaeology.

His paintings have an exacting quality, evident in the clarity of the drawing, the contours of the figures and objects, and his use of bright colours. The work displays a complicated iconography, in which the fruits and garlands that adorn his work play a part.

Crivelli's works are exclusively of religious subjects. They tend to be elaborate, betraying a Venetian love of pageantry and ornamentation. Ringing colours, dominated by metal and stone, are typical. The ornate domestic setting and the grandeur of the architecture of *The Annunciation* reflects a civic pride and a close attention to detail and perspective.

 Pietà, Madonna and Child Enthroned, Madonna della Candeletta

Giovanni Bellini (c. 1430–1516)

Madonna of the Small Trees
Accademia Gallery, Venice. Courtesy of the Bridgeman Art Library

GIOVANNI BELLINI was first active in about 1445. Although he was trained by his father Jacopo, his most important influence was Andrea Mantegna. Bellini was known for the soft quality of his work and was an excellent portraitist. He was the civic painter of Venice, and many eminent painters, such as Titian (*c.* 1485–1576) and Giorgione (*c.* 1477–1510), trained in his studio. He, his father and elder brother, Gentile (*c.* 1429–1507), are credited with transforming the art of Venice to rival that of Florence and Rome.

Always open to new ideas, Bellini was influenced by Antonello da Messina to become one of the earliest masters of the oil technique. Oils allowed the linearity of his early work to give way to light and colour as the two most important means of expression.

He was also one of the first artists to create architectural settings for his *sacra conversazione* pieces, so that they appeared to extend in to the space of the real architecture.

In his portraiture, Bellini often used the Flemish three-quarter profile against a landscape. He painted a few mythological and allegorical works but was primarily a religious painter, particularly of Madonnas, and was known for the serenity and sympathy of his figures and for the inventiveness of his designs. This painting shows his precision in rendering light and shade, and his faultless sense of perspective.

 Doge Leonardo Loredan, San Zaccaria altarpiece, *Feast of the Gods*

Andrea del Verrocchio
(Andrea di Cioni) (1435–88)

Monument to Bartolommeo Colleoni
Piazza San Giovanni e Paolo, Venice. Courtesy of the Bridgeman Art Library

ANDREA DEL VERROCCHIO became the leading sculptor in Florence after the death of Donatello. He was trained as a goldsmith, painter and sculptor, and may have been taught by Donatello, but his sculptural style refers more to the Romantic sensitivity of the latter half of the fifteenth century.

Verrocchio's two-statue group of *Christ and St Thomas* (1467–83) was one of the largest to have been commissioned at that time. It was designed to fit into a niche in Orsanmichele, Florence, which had originally been intended for one statue, revealing the artist's versatility. It also shows the lightness, elegance of pose and high craftsmanship for which he was renowned. Verrocchio was frequently commissioned by the powerful Medici family, and most

of the artists who were active around 1490 studied at his workshop. He was Leonardo da Vinci's (1452–1519) master and it is said that he was so overwhelmed by the angel that Leonardo painted in his *Baptism of Christ* that he decided not to paint again. Certainly, after this time, he seems to have concentrated solely on producing his sculpture.

His major sculptural works, which are comparable with works by Donatello, are his *David* (1473–75) and his last commission, the superb equestrian statue of the Venetian warlord Bartolommeo Colleoni, which is still on display in Venice.

 Lady with a Posy, David, Putti Fountain

Sandro Botticelli
(Alessandro di Mariano Filipepi) (c. 1445–1510)

The Birth of Venus
Uffizi Gallery, Florence. Courtesy of the Bridgeman Art Library

SANDRO BOTTICELLI was one of the greatest and most popular Italian masters of the late fifteenth-century. His graceful, rounded style and the projection of a sense of spirituality in his work were the result of an apprenticeship with Filippo Lippi. He later worked with the Pollaiuolo brothers, absorbing their naturalism as well as their techniques of foreshortening and perspective.

Botticelli reacted against the realism of Masaccio by reviving elements of Gothic art – a delicacy of sentiment, expressed in an ornamental style – that he imbued with freshness and beauty. He worked in tempera, usually on panel, and painted portraits as well as religious, political and mythological works full of allegory as well as symbolism.

In 1481 he was called to Rome to paint part of the Sistine Chapel. Returning to Florence in 1484, his style became harsher and he withdrew from public life to illustrate Dante Alighieri's *Inferno*, written in *c.* 1307. During his lifetime, Botticelli's style was viewed as archaic, especially in comparison with Renaissance artists such as Leonardo da Vinci (1425–1519), Raphael (1483–1520) and Michelangelo (1475–1564), and he died in obscurity.

The Medici family, the great Renaissance patrons of Florentine art, commissioned *The Birth of Venus*, showing the Roman goddess of love and beauty rising from the sea on a sculpted sea shell.

Primavera, Adoration of the Magi, The Mystical Nativity

Filippino Lippi (c. 1457–1504)

Portrait of an Old Man
Palazzo Pitti, Florence. Courtesy of the Bridgeman Art Library

FILIPPINO LIPPI was the son and pupil of Fra Filippo Lippi and, after his father's death in 1469, the pupil of Botticelli. His work is often overshadowed by that of his two masters. Filippino's first major commission came in 1484 when he was asked to complete Masaccio's frescoes in the Brancacci Chapel of Santa Maria del Carmine in Florence, which he did with sensitivity. From these works, Lippi first made his name as an artist.

His most important frescoes are those of the *Life of St Thomas Aquinas* (1488–93) in the Caffa Chapel in Santa Maria sopra Minerva, Rome, and the *Lives of St Philip and St John* (1487–1502) in the Strozzi Chapel in Santa Maria Novella, Florence. In these he created picturesque yet dramatic effects which, combined with

a graceful quality, identify him as one of the most inventive of Italy's late fifteenth-century artists.

After a period in Rome, his work showed an increased use of architecture and detail taken from classical painting. Filippino also painted many altarpieces, which are typified by bright, glowing colour. This painting illustrates his robust style. He was a master of expression – note the wrinkles on the old man's face and the resigned posture of his slightly bowed head and crossed arms, all lit from a single light source to the left of the painting.

 The Vision of St Bernard, Virgin and Child, Adoration of the Magi

Gentile Bellini (c. 1429–1507)

The Miracle of the True Cross near San Lorenzo Bridge
Courtesy of the Bridgeman Art Library

GENTILE BELLINI, the elder son of Jacopo Bellini (c. 1400–70), was trained by his father in Venice. His first known work, a portrait of Lorenzo Giustiniani, the first patriarch of the city, dates from 1465. A year later he worked with his father, as well as Bartolommeo Vivarini (1432–99) and Francesco Squarcione, the adopted father of Andrea Mantegna, on a series of frescoes for the Scuola di San Marco in Venice. Soon afterwards he was appointed official portraitist in Venice and between 1479-81, his skills took him to Constantinople as portraitist to Sultan Mehmet II, where he absorbed the influences of eastern, Byzantine-influenced art.

In 1474 Gentile began a series of history paintings in the Council Chamber in the Doge's palace, which were destroyed by fire in 1577. He also produced portrait groups that included views of Venice and a number of large, propaganda-based civic canvases depicting religious incidents from Venice's history. *The Miracle of the True Cross near San Lorenzo Bridge* is one such work. Painted in oil, it is one of three works for the Cycle of the True Cross painted for the Scuola di San Giovanni and is typical for its anecdotal qualities and attention to detail. The painting is suffused with soft light which dwells on the crowd and highlights the stunning Venetian architecture in detail.

Sultan Mehmet II, Procession of the Reliquary of the Cross in the Piazza St Marco, The Miraculous Healing of Pietro de' Ludovici

c. 1480 Domenico Ghirlandaio (1449–94)

Old Man and His Grandson
Louvre, Paris. Courtesy of the Bridgeman Art Library

BORN in Florence, Domenico Ghirlandaio originally trained as a goldsmith; this explains, in part, his highly decorative style and extensive use of gold embellishments. He worked predominantly in the field of fresco painting, and once said that he would like to decorate every wall of every building. He became a highly popular and prolific fresco artist in Florence, receiving many prestigious commissions. He passed on his great skill at fresco painting to his most famous apprentice, Michelangelo (1475–1564).

Many of Ghirlandaio's frescoes, although intended to depict religious narratives, also contain portraits of key figures and patrons of Florence society. A similar personalisation is apparent in his anachronistic settings: fashionable, wealthy Florence is often used as the backdrop for his biblical scenes. The inclusion of contemporary details in frescoes of this era was discredited by some critics of Ghirlandaio as obtrusive and unrealistic; however, this technique helped to give the works more immediacy, bringing the biblical stories into the realm of the artist and viewer of the time.

A key element of Ghirlandaio's success was the realistic detail he applied to his representations of people, a realism that is evident in *Old Man and His Grandson*, in which the master has literally taken the 'warts and all' approach.

 Portrait of a Lady, The Last Supper, Adoration of the Shepherds

EARLY RENAISSANCE

Perugino (Pietro Vannucci) (c. 1445–1523)

Madonna del Sacco
Palazzo Pitti, Florence. Courtesy of the Bridgeman Art Library

THE Umbrian master Perugino was born in Città della Pieve. During the late 1460s he moved to Florence to study with Andrea del Verrochio, the master who also taught Leonardo da Vinci. Perugino's work became highly prized towards the end of the fifteenth century, but a decade later his work was criticised for being repetitious and formulaic. He often reused cartoons, probably due to the large volume of work undertaken by his studios in Perugia and Florence.

From 1481, with Botticelli and Ghirlandaio, Perugino decorated the walls of the Sistine Chapel with fresco paintings depicting scenes from the Old and New Testaments as well as portraits of several popes. Today he is chiefly remembered as Raphael's master.

Certainly Raphael's earliest works were strongly influenced by Perugino, who passed on the technique of using tilted heads to express religious sincerity; and both artists painted luxuriously coloured, sculptural robes which emphasised the classical quality of their gracefully posed figures.

The *Madonna del Sacco* shows two key features of Perugino's work: his figure painting, in the conventional style of Florentine artists of the time; and his use of Umbrian landscapes in earthy colours to form a strong contrast with the brightness of the robes.

The Virgin and Child with Saints, Christ Giving the Keys to St Peter, The Crucifixion

HIGH RENAISSANCE

Leonardo da Vinci (1452–1519)

Mona Lisa
Louvre, Paris. Courtesy of the Bridgeman Art Library

LEONARDO was a formidable genius who, with Michelangelo and Raphael, shaped and accelerated the great changes that took place in the period known as the High Renaissance. Born in 1452 in Tuscany, Leonardo was apprenticed to the sculptor Andrea del Verrocchio. From 1482 he worked at the court of Milan – not solely as an artist, for he possessed great skills and knowledge in many areas: he was a talented scientific investigator, engineer, architect and designer. In Leonardo's final years, his main area of interest lay in natural sciences; many of his workbooks showing intricate scientific and anatomical diagrams have survived. Few of his completed paintings survive, but those that remain show his remarkable talent. Leonardo pioneered many new artistic techniques that were later copied and developed by his contemporaries. One such technique was *sfumato*, meaning to give the appearance of imperceptible changes in gradation of light, so that harsh outlines took on a softened appearance.

This technique was employed in the *Mona Lisa*, arguably the most famous painting in the history of western art, which has become almost an icon to art itself. A serenely smiling woman, whose identity still remains unknown, appears in front of a mist-strewn rocky landscape, which further increases the painting's enigmatic qualities.

 Virgin of the Rocks, Child and St Anne, The Last Supper

HIGH RENAISSANCE

David

Accademia Gallery, Florence. Courtesy of the Bridgeman Art Library

MICHELANGELO was born in Caprese and was apprenticed to the Florentine master Domenico Ghirlandaio. His talents were soon recognised by Lorenzo de' Medici, who took the young artist into his home. While with the Medici family, Michelangelo was able to study their impressive collection of classical antiquities. Such studies clearly had a great impact on his work from the beginning, as seen in his very early pieces such as *The Madonna of the Steps* (1491–92).

Michelangelo's greatest interest lay in sculpture, but it was the series of fresco paintings he carried out on the ceiling of the Sistine Chapel (1508–12), regarded as one of the crowning achievements of the High Renaissance, that ultimately consolidated his fame,

begun with the completion of his sculptural works *Pietà* (1498–9) and *David*. Michelangelo was also a creative architect and talented poet. He was an extremely pious man who never married, living meagrely in Rome until his death in 1564.

Throughout his career Michelangelo sculpted and painted images of young male nudes, beautifully formed and gracefully poised. In *David*, Michelangelo's early study of human anatomy is evident in the superbly realistic form of the young man who stands with sling shot held lightly, waiting for his enemy to come into range.

The Sistine Chapel frescoes, *Pietà*, *The Doni Tondo*

Il Sodoma (Giovanni Bazzi) (1477–1549)

The Descent from the Cross
National Pinacoteca, Siena. Courtesy of the Bridgeman Art Library

GIOVANNI BAZZI, known as Il Sodoma, was born in Lombardy. He was the son of a shoemaker and it was alleged by writers of the time that he earned his nickname because of his homosexuality; if this is true, then it was a name he was pleased with, as he used it in his signature consistently.

In 1490, at the age of 13, Sodoma was apprenticed to Giovanni Spanzotti in Vercelli, where he stayed until 1498 when he moved to Milan. Leonardo da Vinci was working in Milan during the same period and his effect on Sodoma is apparent in the latter's works thereafter, particularly the *sfumato* effect seen in many of his paintings. From 1500 Sodoma was working in Sienna, where the majority of his works were undertaken, and indeed he dominated

the Sienese art scene for several years, although he also worked in Rome. In 1508 Sodoma was among the elite group of artists who were commissioned by the Pope to decorate the Papal rooms at the Vatican.

Considered to be one of Sodoma's best works, *The Descent from the Cross* combines key elements of High Renaissance art: the landscape background was an important feature of much Italian art at the time, as was the naturalistic style of painting with vivid yet plausible colours.

 Marriage of Alexandria and Roxanne, The Madonna Enthroned, The Vision of St Catherine

Giorgione (c. 1477–1510)

The Tempest
Accademia Gallery, Florence. Courtesy of the Bridgeman Art Library

THE life of Giorgione (Giorgio Barbarelli) is largely a mystery. The Italian Renaissance biographer Giorgio Vasari (1511–74) records Giorgione's birth as occurring in either 1477 or 1478 in the town of Castelfranco near Venice. It is known that Giorgione was apprenticed to Giovanni Bellini and that he later collaborated with several other major artists. The veracity of some of his works has been questioned because of these collaborations; also, his untimely death in 1510 meant that unfinished paintings were completed by other artists. Despite his short career and the small number of completed works, Giorgione's impact on art has been both great and lasting. In particular, his influence on Venetian artists was immense – his superb use of colour had a profound effect on his student Titian's (c. 1488–1576) artistic development. The predominance of landscape and its naturalistic portrayal in his work are features that crop up in the work of many later artists.

The Tempest is perhaps Giorgione's most famous painting. The subject matter, like his life, is perplexing. The identity of the naked woman, and the significance of the male figure watching her, are unclear; any interpretation of the piece remains subjective. Such strange and enigmatic themes were unusual in Renaissance art; more commonly, well-known religious or mythical subjects were commissioned and portrayed.

 Three Philosophers, Adoration of the Magi, Laura

Raphael (1483–1520)

The School of Athens

Vatican Museums and Galleries, Rome. Courtesy of the Bridgeman Art Library

BORN in Urbino, Raphael was the son of a painter. He showed artistic talent from a young age, and at 17 was studying with the master Perugino. Raphael was approaching adulthood while the influence on the contemporary art world of Michelangelo and Leonardo was apparent. For several years he lived in Florence, where they were working; Leonardo's influential *sfumato* style can be seen in much of Raphael's work during this period. He had an innate ability to absorb the innovations of other artists; he did not mimic their style but understood and developed their techniques in such a way as to express his own vision.

In 1508 Raphael was summoned to Rome by the Pope, who commissioned him to decorate the private Papal rooms of the Sistine Chapel; concurrently, Michelangelo was working on the ceiling of the chapel. There was some considerable professional rivalry between the two artists. *The School of Athens* was painted in the Stanza della Segnatura at the Vatican. Framed within a superb architectural setting, the philosophers of the ancient world converse; our eye is drawn to the two central figures of Aristotle and Plato. In this painting, Raphael's perfect rendering of the harmonious balance attempted in earlier classical art holds the key to his importance during and after the High Renaissance.

 The Nymph Galatea, La Belle Jardiniere, The Sistine Madonna

Fra Bartolommeo della Porta (c. 1472–1517)

Resurrection of Christ
Accademia Gallery, Florence. Courtesy of the Bridgeman Art Library

FRA BARTOLOMMEO was apprenticed to Cosimo Rosselli (1439–1507) in 1484. He was deeply affected by the puritanical teachings of the controversial Florentine monk Savonarola, after whose death, in 1498, he took holy orders at San Marco monastery in Florence. He then set about destroying all his works containing nudes, considering them sinful, and did not resume painting until 1504, when he became head of the monastery workshop.

His intention in painting was to instill religious devotion in his audience. His works are characterised by a religious intimacy – particularly his Madonnas. He visited Venice in 1508 and Rome in 1514, both visits helping him to develop the balance and simplicity of his paintings. Fra Bartolommeo was one of the first artists to use dress to emphasise the difference between the human and the divine in painting – his religious figures do not wear contemporary clothes.

This *Resurrection of Christ* shows the expressive gestures, rapt expressions and simplicity of setting that are typical of his work. The central figure of Christ dominates the painting, with the aim of inspiring awe, contemplation and worship in the viewer. His *contraposto* (twisted) pose increases the sense of movement in the painting and reveals the artist as a gifted draughtsman.

Virgin Adoring the Child with St Joseph, Vision of St Bernard, Pietà, The Mystic Marriage of St Catherine

Lorenzo Lotto (1480–1557)

Portrait of a Husband and Wife

Hermitage, St Petersburg. Courtesy of the Bridgeman Art Library

LOTTO was born in Venice, where he trained as an artist. However, he was distanced from other Italian artists by his style of painting, which was viewed as unfashionable in an age dominated by the two great Venetian painters, Titian (*c.* 1488–1576) and Tintoretto (1518–94). Lotto was a unique artist, with a vision that enabled him to create remarkable paintings which have a contemporary resonance today. His realistic and empathetic works, filled with distinctive sharp lines and vivid colours, lean towards Flemish art rather than Venetian.

Consequently, during his lifetime Lotto did not achieve the level of success that his accomplished and emotive paintings deserved; he died penniless, having joined a religious order in 1554. For

centuries Lotto remained largely ignored by art critics, and it was only in the twentieth century that his reputation was restored.

Lotto's most successful paintings were portraits. *The Portrait of a Married Couple* is a fine example of his vivid style, not least for its depiction of symbolic objects such as the squirrel and the sheet of paper with the inscription that reads 'Man not animal'. Lotto's penchant for including symbolic references in his paintings has led some to describe him as a forerunner to the Surrealists.

 Andrea Odoni, St Catherine of Alexandria, Portrait of Goldsmith in Three Positions

The Last Supper

Church of François Xavier, Paris. Courtesy of the Bridgeman Art Library

BORN in Venice, Jacopo Tintoretto seldom left the place of his birth. He was given the nickname Il Tintoretto, meaning little dyer, because his father was a cloth dyer. Although he was the most prolific of all the Venetian artists, he did not gain the level of prestige usually attributed to masters – possibly due to his artisan background. To complete the vast number of commissions he accepted, Tintoretto used a large team of apprentices. Moreover, he was known to use unscrupulous means to secure his commissions; both of these facts made him unpopular with his contemporaries.

Tintoretto once described his art as combining the form of Michelangelo with the colour of Titian and, indeed, both elements are present in many of his paintings, from his evident fascination with the body in movement to the rich, deep colours that he employed. Tintoretto was commissioned to paint the familiar scene of *The Last Supper* eight times by various patrons. Here, he has employed a traditional frontal perspective, with the table edge running parallel to the frame, than is seen in his later paintings. The scene is infused with drama by the dynamic portrayal of the agitation of the disciples and the way in which the light falls on their faces, but Christ, surrounded by a soft suffused light, remains very clearly the focal figure of the painting.

 St Mark Rescuing the Slave, Assumption of the Virgin, The Last Supper

Giovanni Battista Moroni (c. 1525–78)

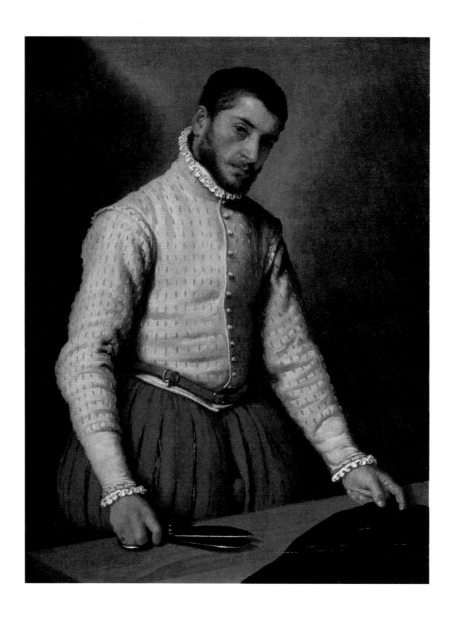

The Tailor
The National Gallery, London. Courtesy of the Bridgeman Art Library

BORN in Bergamo, Moroni moved to Brescia to study with the master Alessandro Moretto (*c.* 1498–1554), whose influence is clear in Moroni's earlier works. The similarity of style between the two is marked and they may have worked together on several paintings. Like most Renaissance artists, Moroni's earlier works are dominated by religious themes as many of the wealthiest art patrons were key figures in the church.

Moroni's fame, however, was due to his remarkable skill at portraiture, a genre in art that became increasingly popular during the Renaissance. His approach to portrait painting was heavily influenced by Lotto, although he evinces a natural realism that is absent in Lotto's works; conversely, Moroni's work does not include symbolic references, nor does it attempt create the level of empathy with the sitter that Lotto achieved. Although it was usual for Renaissance artists to choose aristocratic, wealthy subjects, Moroni used working class subjects in his portraits.

The Tailor has a stark, simple background – a plain wall which concentrates the eye on the subject. The colour is typical of a Brescian artist; low-key, dominated by pale, light browns. The tailor looks directly at us, his tools in his hand – he is what we see, there are no hidden allusions here.

 Portrait of the Duke of Albuquerque, Portrait of a Gentleman, Portrait of a Young Nobleman

Self-Portrait
Private Collection, Milan. Courtesy of the Bridgeman Art Library

SOFONISBA Anguissola was born into a noble family in Cremona, Italy. She was one of four sisters who were all artistically talented. During the sixteenth century in Italy there were perhaps 40 female artists, of whom Anguissola was to gain the most success; during her lifetime her paintings were bought by many great Italian families.

Her talent was recognised at an early age and after her mother died, her liberal father encouraged and supported her, which enabled her to overcome the constraints of sixteenth century life to become a well-known painter. For three years she studied in Cremona under Bernardino Campi, then from about 1549 she studied with the Spanish artist Il Sojaro for a further three years.

Records of her father's letters to Michelangelo about Anguissola exist; in these he asks the master for a sketch by his own hand for Anguissola to paint. Anguissola's skill was spotted by the Duke of Alba in Spain, and soon her talent at portraiture was rewarded by employment as court painter and lady-in-waiting at the court of Queen Isabel of Spain, where she lived for several years. The self-portrait was a genre in which Anguissola excelled. Here, a youthful Anguissola stares out, with a hint of a smile lifting the corners of her mouth and wide-open eyes that imply apprehension.

Holy Family, The Artist's Sisters Playing Chess, Child Bitten by a Crayfish

Paolo Veronese (1528–88)

The Marriage Feast at Cana

Louvre, Paris. Courtesy of the Bridgeman Art Library

PAOLO CALIARI was born in Verona, hence he was known by the name Veronese. He studied with Antonio Badile while living in Verona, before moving to Venice in about 1553. With Titian and Tintoretto, Veronese dominated the Venetian art scene. His use of colour differed from that of other painters of the Venetian school, and hints of his training in Verona can be seen in his distinctive yet harmonious colouring.

Veronese often painted religious scenes, placing them in an incongruous Venetian setting with the saints dressed in finery and jewels. Although he was censored for this decorative element, which some viewed as sacrilegious, it enabled him to portray the splendour of life in the rich and triumphant city-state of Venice.

During the early years of his career in Venice, Veronese painted frescoes for the great architect Sanmicheli. As a result, many of his works convey a lasting impression of the detail of architecture, including *The Marriage Feast at Cana*, where the feast takes place against a magnificent backdrop of sweeping Classical colonnades. The architectural setting intensifies the illusion that the painting is a scene from a play – sixteenth-century theatres often had two such flanking flights of stairs. Veronese has included a self-portrait of himself playing the *viola da braccio*; beside him are fellow artists Titian and Tintoretto.

 The Finding of Moses, Venus and Mars, Perseus and Andromeda

Titian (c. 1488–1576)

Self-Portrait
Prado, Madrid. Courtesy of the Bridgeman Art Library

OF all the Venetian artists who flourished during the sixteenth century, Titian gained the most enduring prestige and renown, his work influenced his contemporaries and generations of oil painters that succeeded him. Although he lived in Venice for almost all of his adult life, his fame brought him eminent patrons in many countries of Europe.

Born in the Dolomites, Titian moved to Venice as a child. He studied with Giovanni and Gentile Bellini, the founders of the Venetian school. He also studied later with Giorgione, completing some of the master's works after his sudden death. Titian's own career was long; he lived into his nineties, creating innovative and impressive art even in his final years. In old age he used his fingers to apply the paint, creating an energy and depth of field that was emulated more than three centuries later by the Impressionists.

Unlike other key artists of the High Renaissance, Titian devoted himself solely to oil painting. His most memorable paintings illustrate religious or mythological scenes but he was also a highly skilled portraitist. This late *Self-Portrait* lacks Titian's usual glorious range of colour. Instead, he depicts himself dressed in black against a shady background, only his face stands out, ghostly amid the darkness where the light falls softly on to it.

Sacred and Profane Love, The Venus of Urbino, Portrait of Charles V

Andrea del Sarto (1486–1530)

Portrait of a Young Man

Palazzo Pitti, Florence. Courtesy of the Bridgeman Art Library

ANDREA DEL SARTO grew up in Florence, which was then the centre of an artistic melting pot. His training was with Piero di Cosimo (*c.* 1462–*c.* 1521), and then he set up a studio with the painter Francesco Franciabigio (*c.* 1482–1525). He also worked with Jacopo Sansovino (1486–1570), with whom he became great friends and occasionally collaborated.

In *c.* 1517 he married a young widow, Lucrezia, of whom he made several portraits. Sometime in 1518–19 he left Florence for the French court of Francis I at Fontainebleau, where he was a great success. He returned to Florence after entreaties from Lucrezia, where he was elected to the prestigious Companies of San Luca and San Sebastiano. Despite his avowed intentions to return to France, he remained in Italy, becoming one of Florence's most respected artists.

Although the vast majority of Del Sarto's work is religious, he painted several portraits, including *Portrait of a Young Man*, and an occasional self-portrait. His work is deeply moving: the eyes of the sitter, like those in his *Christ Redeemer* (1515–16), are haunting in their intensity. The eyes of the young man seem to look directly at the viewer, capturing and holding them spellbound.

 Noli Me Tangere, Birth of the Virgin, Christ Redeemer

The Visitation
San Michele, Carmignano, Prato. Courtesy of the Bridgeman Art Library

PONTORMO, whose real name was Jacopo Carucci, adopted the name of the city of his birth in Italy. As a young man, he moved from his home town to Florence and undertook artistic training under Mannerist master Andrea del Sarto. Through Del Sarto, Pontormo came into contact with Jacopo Sansovino, as well as moving within the same circles as the elderly Leonardo da Vinci and Piero di Cosimo (*c.* 1462–*c.* 1521). His work was also influenced by Michelangelo and Albrecht Dürer (1471–1528).

As an associate of Del Sarto, Pontormo came to the attention of the Medici Grand Duke, Cosimo I (1519–74), who commissioned him to decorate one of his villas with frescoes; he also worked on Lorenzo de' Medici's villa at Poggia a Caiano, as well as the decorations of the Chiostro Grande in Florence's Medici Chapel in preparation for a state visit by Pope Leo X (1475–1521).

Pontormo was a reclusive artist who filled his paintings with dreamlike images. The bright colours, static figures and flowing draperies of *The Visitation* are typical of his style: the far-away look in the eyes of the young woman on the right, the wisps of golden halos and the feet of the two saints that barely seem to touch the ground combine to reinforce the sense of unreality.

 Deposition, Joseph in Egypt, Lady with a Lapdog

Correggio (c. 1490–1534)

Noli Me Tangere
Prado, Madrid. Courtesy of the Bridgeman Art Library

CORREGGIO, whose real name was Antonio Allegri, was born in Correggio, Italy. For most of his life he worked in and around Parma, in an artistic style that bordered High Renaissance and Mannerism. He was strongly influenced by Andrea Mantegna, and followed the older artist's example in painting church domes with a *sotto in sù* effect to create the illusion that the subjects of the painting were floating freely in mid-air. The result is an extremely life-like and realistic effect, as though the scene is actually taking place above our heads. Correggio achieved this wonderful effect after intensive study of the effects of light and shadow; a superb example of his *sotto in sù* work can be seen in the *Assumption* (1526–30) at Parma Cathedral.

Correggio also produced mythological paintings, such as the *Loves of Jupiter* series (c. 1530–33). As well as the influence of Mantegna, his work reveals an indebtedness to Raphael, Leonardo da Vinci and Michelangelo. Correggio's mastery of light can be seen in the glowering sky of *Noli Me Tangere*, which was painted at the end of his life. Correggio' work was hugely influential on the Baroque movement and on the work of Bernini (1598–1680) and Parmigianino (1503–40).

 The Madonna of the Basket, Mercury Instructing Cupid, Assumption of the Virgin

Parmigianino (1503–40)

Madonna with the Long Neck
Uffizi Gallery, Florence. Courtesy of the Bridgeman Art Library

THE painter Girolamo Francesco Maria Mazzola was nicknamed 'Parmigianino' after his home town of Parma in Italy. In 1524 he travelled to Rome, although German occupation in 1527 saw him fleeing from imprisonment to the safety of Bologna. From there he returned to Parma in 1531. As well as oils, Parmigianino produced engravings and frescoes, decorating churches in the cities of Rome, Bologna and Parma.

Parmigianino was a pupil of Correggio, and was also influenced by Raphael and Michelangelo, although he developed a unique style. His works became renowned for their eroticism, unusual perspective, heightened imagination and elongation of the human figure. The latter can be seen in *The Madonna with the Long Neck*,

which caused a contemporary uproar. Parmigianino's intention was to emphasise the Madonna's beauty by giving her an elongated neck – a sign of great beauty and of sexual availability. However, the picture was interpreted as flippant and even blasphemous.

Towards the end of his short life, Parmigianino became obsessed with alchemy, a fixation that seems to have heralded insanity. He was imprisoned (for a second time) for breach of contract when he left the fresco at Santa Maria della Steccata in Parma unfinished. He died aged just 37.

Cupid Carving his Bow, Self-Portrait in a Convex Mirror, The Vision of St Jerome

Agnolo Bronzino (1503–72)

Eleanora of Toledo and Her Son

Uffizi Gallery, Florence. Courtesy of the Bridgeman Art Library

AGNOLO BRONZINO was one of the first generation of Mannerists. He became a court painter and favourite of Duke Cosimo I de' Medici (1519–74) – a generous patron of the arts who also furthered the careers of Benvenuto Cellini (1500–71) and Giorgio Vasari (1511–74).

He was well known as a portrait painter but perhaps his most famous painting is an allegorical scene, *Venus, Cupid, Folly and Time* (c. 1550). He also painted frescoes and produced books of poetry. This portrait is of Cosimo de' Medici's wife, Eleanora, and their son Giovanni de' Medici, one of their eight children. The pattern on Eleanora's dress is exquisitely detailed, as is her hair decoration and the embroidery of Giovanni's collar and cuffs. The white material of the dress is rendered faithfully, gleaming and occasionally dappled by the shadow of its folds. The inscrutable expressions on the faces of both subjects are characteristic of Bronzino's portrait work, which did not seek to reveal the character of the sitters. Instead, he used clarity of colour and a depiction of the richness of the clothes to denote their elevated social status. This, coupled with his obvious talent and fashionable connections, made Bronzino a much sought-after portraitist.

 Venus, Cupid, Folly and Time, Piero de' Medici ('The Gouty'), *Lucrezia Panciatichi*

Giambologna (1529–1608)

The Rape of the Sabine

Loggia dei Lanzi, Florence. Courtesy of the Bridgeman Art Library

GIAMBOLOGNA, the best-known and most important Mannerist sculptor, is sometimes referred to as Giovanni di Bologna or Jean de Boulogne – he was Flemish by birth but relocated to Italy, where his name was Italianised. After initial training in the Netherlands, between *c.* 1545 and 1550, he moved to Rome, where he lived for two years before settling permanently in Florence. Here he was patronised by the Medici ruler Ferdinando I (1549–1609), who commissioned Giambologna to sculpt an enormous equestrian statue of Grand Duke Cosimo I (1519–74), which set a precedent for equestrian-style statues throughout Europe.

Giambologna worked in marble and bronze. His works range in size from small bronzes, such as *Mercury* (*c.* 1565), now in the Bargello, Florence, to the monumental piece that sealed his reputation, *Neptune's Fountain* (1566), in Bologna.

His sculptures were ground-breaking for their apparent ability to defy the laws of gravity and in their portrayal of movement, as seen in *The Rape of the Sabine*. The sculpture, on show in the Loggia de Lanzi in Florence, is much-admired for its fluidity and anatomical accuracy, from the cowering man at the base to the pinnacle provided by the woman's outstretched hand.

Mercury, Hercules and the Centaur, Florence Triumphant over Pisa

1586–88 Domenikos Theotocopoulos 'El Greco' (1541–1614)

The Burial of Count Orgaz
San Tome, Toledo. Courtesy of Index/the Bridgeman Art Library

DOMENIKOS THEOTOCOPOULOS was born in Crete. At the age of 19 he travelled to Italy, spending time in Venice – Crete was currently under Venetian rule – and Rome. In the mid-1570s he moved to Toledo in Spain, where he remained. It was in Toledo that he was given the name 'El Greco', 'the Greek', by which he is still known. He resisted the nickname, however, signing his paintings with his real name, in Greek.

El Greco's early art was Byzantine in style, but he soon became absorbed by the Mannerist style during his protracted sojourn in Spain, and is known as 'the last Mannerist painter'. His works consisted mainly of religious paintings and portraits, such as *Fra Felix Hortensio Paracivino* (c. 1605), although he also painted a number of landscapes and one mythological painting: the splendid *Laocoön* (c. 1610). El Greco was also an architect and sculptor.

The Burial of Count Orgaz is based on a legend which dates back to 1323: the count was a deeply religious and charitable man, of such piety that the saints Augustine and Stephen materialised at his funeral and lowered his body to its resting place. Interestingly, El Greco reinterpreted the myth in his own time, dressing the count and his mourners in sixteenth-century fashions.

 Fra Felix Hortensio Paracivino, The Assumption of the Virgin, El Espolio

Albrecht Dürer (1471–1528)

Portrait of Dürer's Father
Uffizi Gallery, Florence. Courtesy of the Bridgeman Art Library

NORTHERN Renaissance art is commonly viewed as secondary to that of Renaissance Italy, with the notable exception of German artist Albrecht Dürer. He had magnificent technical abilities, synthesising Italian and Northern traditions in a unique and much-imitated style that brought him recognition even in Italy. In 1496 Dürer visited Venice, meeting Gentile Bellini, who greatly influenced his painting. He visited Italy again in 1505–07, assimilating the artistic and humanist innovations of the Renaissance.

Dürer's fame spread with his unsurpassed skill in producing engravings and woodcuts, as evidenced by his celebrated book, *The Apocalypse* (1498). Book illustrations were becoming increasingly popular at this time and, with Dürer's remarkable achievements,

more skilfully accomplished than ever. Many of Dürer's letters, annotations and theories on anatomy and perspective have survived. They reveal an intelligent, educated man ever curious about the world around him. Dürer helped to raise the profile of artists in Germany, where the view of the artist as a lowly craftsman still held sway. Dürer's father was a goldsmith, who trained him in their home town of Nuremberg. Possibly following a technique introduced by Leonardo da Vinci, Dürer has placed the sitter's hands at the front of the painting to intensify the illusion that the viewer is included in the painting.

Self-Portrait, Melancholia I, The Festival of the Rose Garlands

Lucas Cranach the Elder (1472–1553)

Venus with Cupid the Honey Thief

Christie's Images. Courtesy of the Bridgeman Art Library

LUCAS Cranach (known as Cranach the Elder to differentiate him from his sons) was born in Kronach, southern Germany. He learnt painting and engraving skills from his father. Cranach was both a friend and supporter of the religious reformer Martin Luther (1483–1546) and, greatly influenced by Dürer's work, he produced several propaganda woodcuts for the Protestant cause.

At the beginning of the sixteenth century Cranach travelled in Germany and Austria, arriving at Vienna in about 1501. The landscape work he produced here created a lasting impression, contributing to the foundation of the Danube School – a group that focused on the importance of landscape painting, particularly of background landscapes used to reflect the emotions or actions of the people portrayed. From 1508 Cranach worked as a court painter for Frederick the Wise, Elector of Saxony, at Wittenberg. Many of Cranach's finest portraits were of court subjects; his portraits were intensely detailed and highly decorative, full of colour and character.

Venus and the Honey Thief is typical of the paintings for which Cranach is chiefly remembered, in both style and content. Like Cranach's other female nudes, this highly stylised Venus is oddly disproportionate (female models were not used at this time) and has an unearthly quality, exuding a dispassionate aloofness.

 A Princess of Saxony, Venus, Portrait of Martin Luther

The Ambassadors

The National Gallery, London. Courtesy of the Bridgeman Art Library

THE German artist Hans Holbein the Younger worked in his father's workshop in Augsberg before moving to Basel, Switzerland, in 1514. Here in Basel, Holbein gained recognition for his book illustrations, most notably the illustration of the *Luther Bible* in 1522. The Reformation movement, led by Martin Luther, had brought troubled times to Europe, influencing Holbein's decision to move to England in 1526 in search of greater prosperity.

In England, Holbein worked for the high-ranking Sir Thomas More (1478–1535), and his second visit in 1532 led to a portrait commission from King Henry VIII. By 1536 he was working for the King as a painter and costume and jewellery designer. His meticulously detailed court portraits, especially those of the king

himself, secured Holbein's already esteemed reputation. *The Ambassadors* shows the French ambassador on the left, with a friend. They are surrounded by objects that illustrate their social standing and wealth, but the distorted shape of the skull beneath them (which achieves correct perspective when viewed from a side angle) is an indicator of their mortality. *The Ambassadors* contains a wealth of precise and minute detail, a typical feature of Northern Renaissance art that began with Jan van Eyck.

🖎 *Henry VIII, The Artist's Wife with Katherine and Philip, Portrait of Desiderius Erasmus*

Nicholas Hilliard (c. 1547–1619)

Young Man Against a Rose Tree

The Victoria and Albert Museum, London. Courtesy of the Bridgeman Art Library

NORTHERN RENAISSANCE

NICHOLAS HILLIARD was the first English-born painter about whom any significant historical facts were recorded. He was born in Exeter and was trained by his father as a goldsmith, but by the age of 13 was showing remarkable flair at miniature painting. By 1569 Hilliard had become a painter of portraits at the court of Queen Elizabeth I (1558–1603).

While at court, Hilliard continued to use his training as a goldsmith, designing the Queen's second Great Seal in 1584. However, his main recognition came from his skill at painting miniatures, or 'limners', as they were called. By the late sixteenth century the miniature had become a fashionable item and was often worn as jewellery, especially in the royal courts of England and France. Hilliard quoted one of his influences as Holbein the Younger, whose intricately detailed paintings must have yielded much for him to study.

The miniature *Young Man Against a Rose Tree* is intended to demonstrate the sixteenth-century ideals of courtly love. It bears a Latin inscription at the top that reads 'My praised faith causes my suffering'. The man's attire and pose indicate a love-sick young aristocrat, who probably commissioned the miniature as a gift for the woman for whom he pines.

 Queen Elizabeth I, Alice Hilliard, Richard Hilliard

Joachim Patenier (c. 1485–1524)

Charon Crossing the River Styx
Prado, Madrid. Courtesy of the Bridgeman Art Library

JOACHIM PATENIER was born in France but by 1515 had registered as a master in the city of Antwerp. He was a friend of the great German artist Albrect Dürer, whose detailed prints of dark subjects evidently impressed Patenier, for his dramatic paintings often simulate the themes found in Dürer's work.

Patenier's use of landscape changed the direction of Flemish art. During the Renaissance, landscape was increasingly used as the background of a painted scene, particularly in portraits, such as the *Mona Lisa* (1503) by Leonardo da Vinci. The inclusion of landscape became more prominent in works such as Giorgione's *The Tempest* (c. 1508). However, in Patenier's work the landscape eclipsed the subject to become the primary focus. Later artists such

as Pieter Bruegel (1525–69) were influenced by Patenier's work, and landscapes became dominant in sixteenth-century Flemish art.

In *Charon Crossing the River Styx* the narrative is overshadowed by the compelling landscape that Patenier has invented. Charon is seen in his boat moving towards the viewer across an unearthly coloured sea. On his right are the welcoming Elysian Fields, on his left the darkly burning fires of Hell. In his fantastic, supernatural landscape, Patenier combines the Gothic tradition with the skills of a High Renaissance painter.

 St Jerome in a Rocky Landscape, Flight into Egypt, Baptism of Christ

c. 1563 Pieter Bruegel the Elder (c. 1525–69)

The Tower of Babel

Kunsthistorisches Museum, Vienna. Courtesy of the Bridgeman Art Library

NAMED after his home village in the Netherlands, Pieter Bruegel founded a dynasty of painters. Alongside Dürer, he was the most outstanding Northern European Renaissance artist. Bruegel did not try to assimilate the artistic ideals of the Italian Renaissance – the classical imagery or the harmonious balance and idealised beauty. Instead his artistic direction owes more to his compatriots Bosch (c. 1450–1516) and Patenier. From Bosch, Bruegel took elements of the Gothic and the fantastical to incorporate into his paintings while he followed Patenier's lead in his keen observation of landscape.

Bruegel's portrayals of a seasonally changing landscape usually contained groups of detailed figures, shown hunting, skating across frozen rivers or stumbling through the landscape in drunken festivity. The landscape dominates all these works and the inclusion of tiny figures infers the triviality of man as he battles against the forces of nature. In several paintings he depicted scenes of peasant life; his interest in the lower classes (to which he did not belong) earned him the nickname 'Peasant Bruegel'.

Bruegel often took a moral viewpoint in his work, and here retells the biblical story of the Tower of Babel: God's devastation of a city for its attempt to build a tower that reached to heaven.

 Hunters in the Snow, Peasant Wedding Feast, The Blind Leading the Blind

Jan Bruegel the Elder (1568–1625)

Vase of Flowers
Kunsthistorisches Museum, Vienna. Courtesy of the Bridgeman Art Library

JAN BRUEGEL the Elder was the son of Pieter Bruegel the Elder. Several other members of the Bruegel family were painters, but only Jan found a level of recognition approaching that of his father. His sons also followed the family tradition and became artists, continuing the Bruegel dynasty.

Like his father, Jan travelled in Italy, where he became a member of the prestigious Guild of Rome. He showed great skill in miniature details and so was commissioned to make many cabinet paintings. Jan also collaborated with a number of other painters, including Peter Paul Rubens (1577–1640).

However, it was Jan Bruegel's landscapes that brought him lasting recognition, helping to intensify the existing tradition of Dutch landscape painting in the seventeenth century. Scenes such as the *Garden of Eden* (c. 1602), filled with naturalistic details in a lush profusion of flora and fauna, are typical of his style.

Jan was given the nickname 'Velvet Bruegel' because of the high level of finish employed in his paintings. Despite his success with landscapes, he was regarded as the greatest flower painter of his day, and produced exquisite still life studies such as *Vase of Flowers*, in which his consummate skill in rendering different textures and capturing the light is evident.

The Garden of Eden, A Basket of Flowers, Still Life of Flowers

Heindrick Avercamp (1585–1634)

A Winter Scene with Skaters by a Windmill

Johnny van Haeften Gallery, London. Courtesy of the Bridgeman Art Library

THE Dutch landscape painter Heindrick Avercamp is believed to have been deaf and was known as 'the mute of Kampen'. He spent most of his life in Kampen, a small town set beside a canal in the province of Zuider Zee in the north of Holland. From his style of painting, it is likely that at some time he trained with David Vinckboons (1576–1632) of the Bruegel school. Throughout his career, Avercamp's style of painting did not change. Neither did his subject matter alter greatly – a wintry landscape set beside a frozen canal or river, with minute figures scurrying around. The apparent restriction in his range could be explained by Avercamp's lack of contact with other artists in the major artistic centres that were blossoming elsewhere in the Netherlands.

Avercamp's paintings show us captured moments of time in a small, seventeenth-century Dutch town. His wintry scenes are busy with many small figures of townspeople in various pursuits, such as fishing, skating or, as in *A Winter Scene with Skaters*, playing golf or curling on the ice. Here, the distant figures are minuscule, painted with the same intense detail as a miniature. Avercamp was following a long tradition in Northern European art of paying close attention to small details to enhance the overall effect of the picture.

 A Scene on the Ice Near a Town, Winter Scene on a Canal, Wintry Landscape

Giuseppe Arcimboldo (1527–93)

Spring
Private Collection, Brussels. Courtesy of the Bridgeman Art Library

ARCIMBOLDO, the son of a painter, was born in Milan to a well-connected family. He began his career making stained-glass windows and designing frescoes as well as painting; in later years he concentrated solely on the latter.

In 1562, Arcimboldo travelled to Vienna to the Habsburg court of Ferdinand I. He was to become a court favourite, spending more of his life travelling within the Habsburg Empire, in particular to Vienna and Prague, than in his native country. He returned to Milan for the last decade of his life.

Grotesque allegories such as *Spring* brought Arcimboldo much acclaim in his lifetime, and were often imitated. The original meaning of the term 'grotesque', as applied to art, is a picture whose subject is created from other forms, in this case fruit, vegetables and flowers. After his death, Arcimboldo's popularity faded and his subject matter was treated with derision. It was not until the twentieth century, and the development of Surrealism, that his fame was revived. Salvador Dalí (1904–89), in particular, was strongly influenced by Arcimboldo.

Spring forms part of Arcimboldo's 'Four Seasons' series, and is typical of much of his work. His use of colour is precise and accurate, as is his brushwork.

 Rudolf II as Vertumnus, Self-Portrait, Summer

Annibale Carracci (1560–1609)

Portrait of a Man Drinking
Private Collection, Scotland. Courtesy of the Bridgeman Art Library

ANNIBALE CARRACCI was the younger brother of Agostino Carracci (1557–1602) and the cousin of Lodovico Carracci (1555–1619). The trio set up one of the most successful studios of their time, exporting works across Europe. Annibale is generally considered the most talented of the three, but together the group combined formidable artistry and business acumen.

Lodovico undertook the training of his two younger cousins, schooling them in his own anti-Mannerist views and style. Their collaborative frescoes for the Palazzo Fava, completed in 1584, were, in turn, denounced by the Mannerists.

In his twenties, Annibale moved away from his anti-Mannerist stance, forging ahead with a new style in to which he melded elements of Mannerism and Baroque, as well as influences from Titian (*c*. 1487–1576) and Veronese (*c*. 1528–88). One of his most important works was the decoration of the Palazzo Farnese in Rome (1597–1604).

Carracci was also an important oil painter and portraitist. The rough brushwork and style of *Man Drinking* is evocative of *The Beaneater* (c. 1580–90). In contrast, his painting of *c*. 1601–02, *Domine, quo Vadis?*, is more finished, executed with sharper brushstrokes and better defined facial features. In the latter work he has returned to a more Classical style.

🐚 *The Lamentation of Christ, Venus and Anchises, The Beaneater*

Michelangelo Merisi da Caravaggio (1571–1610)

1606

Supper at Emmaus

Pinacoteca di Brera, Milan. Courtesy of the Bridgeman Art Library

CARAVAGGIO'S early education was undertaken in Lombardy, under the tutelage of Simone Peterzano, who had studied under Titian (*c.* 1487–1576). Around 1592, Caravaggio left Lombardy for Rome, seeking artistic fame. He began his career in Rome as a painter of portraits, as well as spending time perfecting the genres of still life and historical painting.

Caravaggio spent much of his life travelling in Europe – partly because he had an incendiary temper which often got him into trouble. On more than one occasion he was forced to move on after becoming involved in some brawl or other; in 1606 he fled Rome in fear of his life after a gambling disagreement ended in his adversary's death.

By 1600 he had become increasingly interested in religious subjects. In *Supper at Emmaus*, he uses the techniques developed in his earlier work. The penetrating study of Jesus as an ordinary man is central to the painting, while the shocked faces and gestures of the disciples are portrayed with startling, harrowing immediacy by Caravaggio's skilled use of *chiaroscuro* (light and shade). The fruit and bread on the table are painted as carefully as in a still life.

Caravaggio died in prison of a fever – ironically after being arrested for a crime that he did not commit.

Beheading St John the Baptist, The Lute-Player, The Card Sharps

BAROQUE

Judith Slaying Holofernes
Uffizi Gallery, Florence. Courtesy of the Bridgeman Art Library

ARTEMISIA was the daughter of wealthy Orazio Gentileschi (1563–c. 1639), a Mannerist painter patronised by the Florentine Medicis and the Duke of Buckingham in England. Orazio taught his daughter to paint directly on to the canvas, and their styles are extremely similar. Artemisia was influenced by Mannerism, in particular by Bronzino (1503–72) and Pontormo (1494–1556). Orazio hired painter Agostino Tassi to assist in the education of his daughter. In 1611, Tassi raped Artemisia, after which he was arrested, tried publicly and subsequently imprisoned. Artemisia then married and moved to Florence.

It seems likely that Artemisia chose the theme of *Judith Slaying Holofernes* as a result of her painful experience: in the painting,

Holofernes clearly intends to rape Judith, who can be seen exacting her revenge. Artemisia returned to the theme in around 1625, with another jubilant portrayal of a strong, determined woman in *Judith and her Maidservant with the Head of Holofernes*. The subject had been executed by two other artists whom Artemisia greatly admired: Caravaggio and Botticelli.

Artemisia was remarkable for being the only female artist in Italy to be taken seriously at this time. Towards the end of her life she became the first woman to gain admittance to the Accademia del Disegno in Florence.

 Susanna and the Elders, Self-Portrait, Judith and her Maidservant

St Sebastian

Dulwich Picture Gallery, London. Courtesy of the Bridgeman Art Library

RENI was a celebrated figure in his own lifetime. When his tutor Lodovico Carracci (1555–1619) died, Reni took over his studio, inheriting an already secured fortune and reputation. Works of art from Carracci's studio had long been in demand throughout Europe, and this continued under Reni.

Reni took much of his inspiration from Caravaggio (1571–1610) and Raphael (1483–1520); however, the overriding influence on his work was his own quest for beauty and perfection. He took great pains to re-create the colours of his subject exactly and to reproduce faithfully the facial idiosyncracies of his models. These aesthetic values also affected his personal life; contemporary reports survive of his impeccable attire and strict moral beliefs.

The facial expression of St Sebastian recalls Reni's impassioned *Head of Christ* (c. 1640). St Sebastian was a favourite subject of the Renaissance and his popularity continued in the ensuing centuries. Other than the method of his death by arrow, very little is known about the life of the saint, although various legends abound. He was particularly popular with Italian artists because he was believed to have been a native of Milan who was martyred in Rome. His body is reputed to be buried beneath the Appian Way.

 St Jerome and the Angel, The Massacre of the Innocents, Aurora

BAROQUE

Glorification of the Reign of Pope Urban VIII

Palazzo Barberini, Rome. Courtesy of the Bridgeman Art Library

PIETRO DA CORTONA was born Pietro Berettini, but was better known by the name of his birthplace, Cortona, in Italy. He moved to Florence in 1613, where he was greatly influenced by the work of Michelangelo (1475–1564). Cortona is credited with the invention of the High Baroque style of ceiling painting, a technique that was to bring him great fame within his lifetime. Cortona was not only a fresco artist, but also an accomplished painter in oils and an architect. His architectural works include the churches of Santa Maria della Pace (1656–57) and Santi Martina e Luca (1635) in Rome.

The Glorification of the Reign of Pope Urban VIII was created for the ceiling of the Palazzo Barberini, in Rome, which contained more frescoes than any other building in Rome at the time. The Barberini family were Cortona's most generous patrons – another of their commissions included the frescoes in the church of Santa Bibiana (1624–26).

Cortona's architectural training can be distinguished here in the mathematically accurate execution of the 'marble columns', around which the painted figures are grouped. His mastery of light and colour is evident in the halo held by the angel, which seems to glow.

Church of Santa Maria della Pace, *The Holy Family Resting on the Flight to Egypt,* frescoes in Santa Bibiana

Nicolas Poussin (1594–1665)

Et in Arcadia Ego
Louvre, Paris. Courtesy of the Bridgeman Art Library

NICOLAS POUSSIN was arguably the most influential French painter of the seventeenth century. His life was spent alternating between his native country and Rome, where he spent much of his time seeking inspiration in rural areas outside the city.

Poussin's work, which was to influence successive generations of painters, was influenced by that of Raphael, among others. He was unhappy at first with the excesses of the Baroque style, preferring to draw inspiration from the Mannerist style, but his individual Classical style became more empathetic with the Baroque style as his career developed. Poussin was also influenced by great works of literature, particularly those of antiquity. Many of his works illustrate Greek or Roman myths and scenes from the Old Testament, such as *The Worship of the Golden Calf* (*c.* 1635) and *The Gathering of the Manna* (1639).

Scenes of an Arcadian idyll were especially popular subjects for Poussin. Here, a group of shepherds are attempting to decipher the words 'Et in Arcadia Ego' inscribed on the tomb in the centre of the painting. The words are intended to indicate the presence of death even in the most idyllic surroundings. The painting is a reworking of an earlier one entitled *Shepherds of Arcady* (*c.* 1630).

 The Triumph of Pan, The Massacre of the Innocents, Inspiration of the Poet

BAROQUE

Claude Lorrain
(Claude Gellée) (c. 1600–82)

The Embarkation of St Ursula
The National Gallery, London. Courtesy of the Bridgeman Art Library

CLAUDE LORRAIN (born Claude Gellée) left his native France at the age of 14 and travelled to Italy, where he settled in Rome. He specialised in the genre of landscape painting, and showed little interest in figure work. In his paintings the people are vastly overshadowed by the landscape, as in *The Embarkation of St Ursula* and *Landscape with Cephalus and Procris Reunited by Diana* (1645).

Lorrain often painted in the open air and was entranced by the idea of Arcadia. He reputedly spent months at a time living among shepherds and tramps to gain the inspiration for his paintings. His landscapes adhere closely to a pastoral ideal, in which people constitute only a small part of a much greater whole. Lorrain often employed studio assistants to paint in the people in his works, while he concerned himself solely with the landscape.

Here St Ursula is almost insignificant, despite such prominence in the title. The legend tells of a British princess who fled her father's house to avoid marrying against her will. She took 11,000 maids with her and, collectively, they became known as the Virgin Martyrs. Ursula and her maids visited Rome to pay allegiance to the pope but, on the return journey from Rome, they were martyred by a horde of Huns in Cologne.

 Seaport at Sunrise, Landscape with Apollo and Mercury, Landscape with Cephalus and Procris Reunited by Diana

BAROQUE

1645-53 Gianlorenzo Bernini (1598–1680)

Ecstasy of St Teresa of Ávila

Santa Maria della Vittoria, Rome. Courtesy of the Bridgeman Art Library

GIANLORENZO BERNINI – sculptor, painter, designer and architect – was the son of a highly accomplished Mannerist sculptor, Pietro Bernini (1562–1629). Although influenced by his father's work, Gianlorenzo was firmly of his own era and was instrumental in the move from Mannerism to Baroque art. It is largely due to the prevalence of Bernini's works in Rome that the city has such a prominently Baroque style.

His surviving work in Rome includes Piazza Navona's *Fountain of the Four Rivers* (1648–51) and several aspects of St Peter's Basilica in the Vatican. Bernini's ability to make solid marble appear as flowing drapery, as well as his obvious skill in facial portraiture, was unsurpassed.

St Teresa is one of Bernini's most famous works. It is set in fantastically ornate marble surroundings of the Cornaro Chapel, and is a focal point for visitors to the church of Santa Maria della Vittoria in Rome. Teresa was a mystic, nun and religious reformer who lived between 1515 and 1582. The sculpture depicts one of her famous ecstasies, in which God sends an arrow of golden flame into her heart. The arrow in the angel's hand is accentuated by the golden rods behind and above the marble figures.

Constanza Bonarelli, The Rape of Proserpine, The tomb of Pope Alexander VII

Sir Peter Paul Rubens (1577–1640)

Samson and Delilah
The National Gallery, London. Courtesy of the Bridgeman Art Library

FLEMISH painter Rubens received a classical education, and his travels in Italy at the beginning of the seventeenth century furthered his interest in the work of the Renaissance and Venetian masters. He was also a successful and well-respected ambassador, serving diplomatic assignments in Spain, France, England and Holland. He was knighted for his efforts by Charles I in 1630.

Rubens was the leading figure of the Flemish Baroque school. His subjects included religious and mythological scenes as well as hunting scenes and portraits; he excelled in all these genres. His work is characterised by a sense of drama that was typical of the Baroque period, suffused with energetic movement, naturalistic light and glowing, captivating colours.

Obviously inspired by his visits to Italy, Rubens' sumptuous and bold colours emulate those of the great Venetian master Titian (*c.* 1488–1576). The influence of another Italian master, Michelangelo (1475–1564) is evident in *Samson and Delilah*. The body of Samson is painted with the same muscular, sculptural quality as the prophets in Michelangelo's frescoes for the Sistine Chapel (1508–12). Rubens' depiction of light in the piece emphasises his unequalled mastery in the portrayal of real skin and luxurious cloth.

 The Three Graces, The Judgement of Paris, The Apotheosis of Henry IV

Frans Hals (c. 1582–1666)

The Laughing Cavalier
Wallace Collection, London. Courtesy of the Bridgeman Art Library

FRANS HALS lived in Haarlem for most of his life. In 1616 he found fame with a group portrait of Dutch civic guards, and many portrait commissions followed. Today Hals' portraits, with an expressive energy partly derived from his furious brushwork, are viewed as second only to Rembrandt's (1606–69). Unusually for an artist of the Baroque period, Hals' technique is spontaneous and instinctive; he pays scant attention to finish and fine detail, preferring to capture a fleeting moment.

Hals was one of the original pioneers of the *alla prima* technique of painting directly on to the canvas, which, much later, earned the admiration of the Impressionists. His work was not highly regarded during his lifetime, however, and he died in poverty,

largely unknown. Possibly because of Hals' brusque style of painting and often jovial eye, his commissions declined, even though his later works show a greater sobriety and darker colours.

While Rembrandt attempted to portray his subjects' emotions, Hals animated the faces of his models with particular expressions, giving the viewer a superficial glimpse of the person at a certain moment. His poses were informal and often included an expressive gesture – devices that helped the viewer engage with the subject, as with the barely contained mirth of *The Laughing Cavalier*.

The Witch of Haarlem, The Regents of the Haarlem Old Men's Alms House, Elderly Woman

Charles I of England

The National Gallery, London. Courtesy of the Bridgeman Art Library

VAN DYCK was born in Antwerp, northern Belgium. He was an artistically precocious child and was apprenticed by the age of 10. By the age of 17, he already had his own studio. From 1618 to 1621 he was chief assistant to Rubens, who taught Van Dyck to refine his already accomplished use of paint so that, by the 1620s, his painting style had become more precise and fluent.

Van Dyck produced mythological and religious paintings in addition to his many court portraits, but it was in the latter that he excelled. Van Dyck's portrait style, while influenced by Rubens and Titian, is essentially an expression of his own interpretation of the essence of aristocratic blood; the sitters appear aloof and superior, with an other-worldly aura.

The artists moved to London in 1632, where he was knighted by King Charles I (1600–1649) and became portrait artist at his court. Van Dyck painted many portraits of the King, showing him in various poses that were intended to indicate different facets of his sovereignty. Here, Charles is in warrior pose, wearing full armour and seated on a charger. The background landscape is suitably atmospheric, with an evening light that enhances the glowing colours of the horse and the sheen of metal armour.

 Charles I in Hunting Dress, Samson and Delilah, Marchesa Elena Grimaldi

Jacob van Ruisdael (1628–82)

Landscape with Windmills
Dulwich Picture Library, London. Courtesy of the Bridgeman Art Library

CONSIDERED the greatest of the seventeenth-century Dutch landscape painters, Jacob van Ruisdael was born in Haarlem into a family of landscape painters. He was probably taught to paint by his father and uncle. During the 1650s Van Ruisdael travelled around Holland and into northern Germany; these travels furnished him with a wealth of images to re-create.

He painted every aspect of the Dutch landscape, from canals and windmills to villages, cityscapes and mountains. His expressive depictions of the beauty of nature revitalised the landscape genre and inspired later Romantic painters.

Van Ruisdael's paintings often have a note of melancholy, portraying scenes of isolated splendour; crumbling buildings, fallen trees and other objects of decay increase this perception. The artist shows the dramatic majesty of nature while acknowledging its destructive potential. Although most of his paintings spring from reality, Van Ruisdael also constructed images of his own invention.

The use of light and shade was an essential ingredient in his atmospheric, emotionally intense landscapes. In *Landscape with Windmills*, the thick clouds hang ominously over the imposing forms of the windmills, which dominate the painting, reducing the cottages, trees and small figures in the foreground to almost total insignificance.

 The Watermill, Bentheim Castle, The Jewish Cemetery

Jan Steen (1625–79)

Skittle Players Outside an Inn
The National Gallery, London. Courtesy of the Bridgeman Art Library

STEEN was born in Leiden but moved frequently, working in many Dutch towns including the Hague, Delft and Haarlem. He studied with Jan van Goyen (1596–1656), whose daughter he married in 1649. His father was a brewer, and in 1654, when it became impossible to live on his meagre artist's income, he also became an inn-keeper. He did not gain wide recognition in his own lifetime and hundreds of unsold paintings were found after his death.

Steen is mainly known for his scenes of everyday life (genre paintings), many of which illustrate morals, following a tradition set by Bruegel and Bosch. These paintings show the artist's lively sense of humour and irony; he often included portraits of himself in various guises. The incidental details and smaller tableaux taking place behind and around the initial viewpoint are a particular feature of Steen's paintings.

In the *Skittle Players Outside an Inn*, Steen displays his mastery of colour in the portrayal of a lazy summer's day. Like many of his paintings, the scene is one of leisure and merriment. This jovial attitude to his subject matter, possibly a result of his work as an inn-keeper, has meant that Steen is not taken as seriously as his work merits.

The Young Ones Chirrup as the Old Ones Sing, The Feast of St Nicholas, Self-Portrait as a Lutenist

Carel Fabritius (1622–54)

The Goldfinch
Mauritshuis, Hague. Courtesy of the Bridgeman Art Library

CAREL PIETERSZ, known as Fabritius, was born in a small town near Amsterdam. In the 1640s he and his brother studied with Rembrandt (1606–69). Carel was Rembrandt's most outstanding apprentice and is regarded by art historians as the link between Rembrandt and Vermeer (1632–75).

Fabritius settled in Delft in 1650, co-founding the Delft School of painting, of which Vermeer later became the leading exponent. He died tragically early, in the 1654 gunpowder explosion in Delft. It is believed that much of his work was destroyed with him; only about a dozen of his paintings survive.

With his move to Delft, Fabritius turned away from the historical narratives favoured by his master, instead moving towards portraits, still life and the seventeenth-century Dutch tradition of genre painting, in which he depicted scenes of ordinary people.

The Goldfinch is Fabritius's most popular painting. In it he explores the tonal implications of placing a dark object against a light background (the opposite was true of Rembrandt). The brushwork, like that of Rembrandt, is changeable, alternating between a thick concentration and light strokes. The painting shows Fabritius's interest in expressing daylight naturally and convincingly, a technique that was further refined by Vermeer.

 The Raising of Lazarus, Self-Portrait, The Sentry

FLEMISH BAROQUE

1659

Harmensz van Rijn Rembrandt (1606–69)

Self-Portrait

Prado, Madrid. Courtesy of the Bridgeman Art Library

THE Dutch painter Rembrandt was born in Leiden, the son of a miller. He attended Leiden University for a while before abandoning his studies to become an artist's apprentice. In 1625, after six months studying in Amsterdam, Rembrandt returned to Leiden as an independent master. In about 1631 he settled in Amsterdam, where he was highly esteemed, especially for his portraits and historical group paintings. Rembrandt's wealth and happiness were short lived; by the end of the 1640s his wife and three of his four children had died, and by 1658 he was bankrupt. These personal tragedies are reflected in his later work; the drama of his early paintings disappears as he focuses ever more on the emotional, rather than the physical, moments of his narratives.

In Rembrandt's lifetime the Baroque style was the favoured mode of artistic expression. Unlike his contemporary Rubens (1577–1640), Rembrandt did not adhere to the ideals of the Italian Renaissance, choosing instead to focus on the reality of the human condition. Although his earliest works reflect the drama and ornamentation of the Baroque style, Rembrandt's interests lay in exploration of the human psyche. His work was expressive and emotionally literate, capturing the personality of his subjects and baring his emotions in numerous self-portraits such as this one.

 The Anatomy Lesson of Dr Nicholaes Tulp, Blinding of Samson, Return of the Prodigal Son

Woman and a Maid with a Pail in a Courtyard

Hermitage, St Petersburg. Courtesy of the Bridgeman Art Library

BORN in Rotterdam, Pieter de Hooch moved to Delft in 1654, where he is recorded as both painter and manservant to a rich merchant. In Delft he came into contact with Fabritius (1622–54) and Nicholaes Maes (1632–93), both early members of the Delft School. De Hooch depicted scenes of middle-class domestic life, portraying Dutch ideals of domesticity. Jan Vermeer (1632–75) soon added to this genre and, with his greater skill, overshadowed him. By 1667 De Hooch had settled in Amsterdam, where he portrayed subjects from the upper classes, but his later paintings were less successful. He died in an insane asylum in 1684.

De Hooch's paintings have complex structures, which create the illusion of real perspective. Rectangular architectural frames and blocks give the impression of distance, and lead the viewer's eye to the main focus of the painting, such as the two women by the canal in *Woman and a Maid with a Pail*. The receding floor tiles also help to create this impression of perspective.

As well as his mastery of perspective, De Hooch was skilled in the portrayal of natural light falling on a scene. His light is warm – more intense than Vermeer's – and his colour range is richer, with fewer cool tones.

A Maid with a Child in a Courtyard of Delft, Woman Peeling Apples, Two Women beside a Linen Chest

Jan Vermeer (1632–75)

Woman Holding a Jug
MOMA, New York. Courtesy of the Bridgeman Art Library

IT IS believed that Jan Vermeer worked primarily as an art dealer. Little is known of his life and only around 35 paintings can definitely be attributed to him. He achieved little recognition for his own art and died in poverty at the age of 43, leaving a widow and 11 children. It was not until the 1860s and the resurgence of interest in artistic naturalism that Vermeer gained critical acclaim. He created his extremely realistic images using several techniques, including the 'camera obscura' (based on the same principles as early photography).

Vermeer is best known for scenes of everyday domestic life, exemplified by such paintings as the *Young Woman with a Water Jug*. The painting shows us a moment frozen in time – there is a stillness, a lack of action that increases the feeling that we are peeping into the hidden, interior life of another person. The aura of calm that pervades many of Vermeer's paintings is generated by his predominant use of cool blues and yellows. He shows us the scene with a detached but somehow ennobling light, as if attempting to show us the dignity and poetry of the woman's life. The woman's pose and the superbly natural light coming through the open window enhance this feeling.

 The Love Letter, Girl Asleep at a Table, The Lacemaker

Meindert Hobbema (1638–1709)

The Avenue at Middelharnis
The National Gallery, London. Courtesy of the Bridgeman Art Library

HOBBEMA was a student of Van Ruisdael during the late 1650s. He was a landscape painter of considerable skill, with an eye for detail that later made his paintings popular with English painters of the eighteenth and nineteenth centuries. In 1668 Hobbema married and became an excise officer in Amsterdam; his output declined thereafter.

While his work was indebted to that of Van Ruisdael, Hobbema brought his own values and insights to the Dutch landscape genre. Hobbema's style is close to that of Van Ruisdael but veers away from the high drama of his master's works, instead painting peaceful, gentle scenes of an idyllic countryside. His use of light is integral to this difference in style – Hobbema's landscapes are sunnier, more expansive and less oppressive. Van Ruisdael's sense of isolation is not found in Hobbema's work, which frequently includes figures, both human and animal.

Hobbema was faithful to the reality of the landscape and did not include fictional enhancements, which may explain his limited range; he is best known for his numerous paintings of mills. His most famous painting, *The Avenue at Middelharnis*, with elegant trees and a spacious, flat landscape, was especially appealing to the Baroque palette.

 The Mill, A Woody Landscape with a Cottage, Road on a Dyke

Jusepe de Ribera (1591–1652)

St Paul the Hermit
Prado, Madrid. Courtesy of the Bridgeman Art Library

IN 1616, Jusepe de Ribera – also known as José de Ribera and 'lo Spagnoletto' (the little Spaniard) – moved from his native Spain to Naples, in Italy, which was then under Spanish rule. He studied such great Italian masters as Caravaggio (1571–1610) and Correggio, and his early work, in particular, shows their influence in the use of *chiaroscuro* (contrast of light and shadow). Ribera went on to develop his own artistic style, which often included depictions of harsh social realism and portrayals of religious piety and suffering.

De Ribera's subjects dealt with martyrdom and other religious themes, although he also painted non-religious subjects and, occasionally, mythologies. *St Paul and the Hermit* is evocative of his earlier paintings, such as *The Martyrdom of St Bartholomew* (c. 1630), in its sombre realism. The wasting muscles, sagging skin and heavily lined face predicate the hastening end of St Paul's life. It is a poignant portrayal of a saint who is more usually represented by his religious fervour and passion. The rushes he wears, the colour and texture of which seem to meld with the dirt beneath him, intimate that he is soon to be part of the earth. Similarly, his fixed gaze is aimed at the skull, which was a common artistic metaphor indicating human mortality.

 The Clubfooted Boy, St Peter Repentant, Apollo and Marsyas

Diego Rodriguez de Silva y Velázquez (1599–1660)

Las Meninas or The Family of Philip IV
Prado, Madrid. Courtesy of the Bridgeman Art Library

VELÁZQUEZ was born in Seville and moved to Madrid in 1622. He visited Italy several times, but always returned to Madrid, establishing himself as the foremost artist of the Spanish School. He was influenced by Titian (c. 1487–1576), Tintoretto (1518–94) and Veronese (c. 1528–88); he was also great friends with Rubens (1577–1640), who became his travelling companion.

Although Velázquez painted mainly portraits after his royal appointment, he remained interested in other genres; the harsh realities of everyday life, for example are encapsulated in his early works The Water Carrier of Seville (c. 1618) and An Old Woman Cooking Eggs (c. 1618). Las Meninas is also known as The Family of Philip IV. The artist was a favourite of the Spanish King Philip IV, who appointed him as court painter when Velázquez was still only aged 24. Las Meninas not only shows the royal family (Philip and his wife are reflected in the mirror from the artist's canvas), but also Velázquez himself, apparently looking beyond his easel towards the viewer.

The central child in the portrait is the Infanta Margarita, attended by all her maids. Note the female dwarf to the right of the picture. Dwarves were a common theme in Velázquez's paintings, as many were employed in Philip's royal household, mainly as entertainers.

The Rokeby Venus, The Immaculate Conception, King Philip IV

St Francis of Assisi

Art Museum of Catalunya, Barcelona. Courtesy of the Bridgeman Art Library

ZURBARÁN was a painter of the Spanish School and, through Velázquez's recommendation, was employed as a court painter for King Philip IV in Madrid: in the 1630s, Zurbarán decorated Philip's new palace there. Despite this prestigious commission, he spent most of his life in Seville, where he was honoured as one of the city's 'official' painters.

His *oeuvre* spanned mythologies, still life painting and historical scenes. The bulk of his work, however, comprised portraits and religious works – *St Francis of Assisi* encompassed both genres. According to legend, St Francis returned to his tomb after his death, where he was observed standing upright, in the attitude as portrayed by Zurbarán in this painting. The frightening aspect of the saint's face, with its heavenward-staring eyes and parted lips, underlines the fact that this is indeed a corpse.

St Francis is identified by the brown habit worn by Franciscan monks (although the saint himself was not a priest) and by the stigmata, as evidenced by the blood seeping through his robe. Interestingly, Zurbarán has painted the wound over the heart, rather than in the more usual location lower down the torso, towards the waist.

 The Labours of Hercules series, *The Carthusian Saints*, *St Serapion*

Bartolomé Esteban Murillo (1618–82)

Ecce Homo

Caylus Anticuario, Madrid. Courtesy of the Bridgeman Art Library

UNUSUALLY for an artist, Murillo found fame in his own lifetime. In his twenties, he created a series of paintings (1645–46) for the Franciscan Friary in his native Seville, which was an important artistic centre at this time. The 11 paintings depicting Franciscan saints brought him to the attention of the art establishment, and led to many commissions. Murillo became renowned for his religious and sentimental scenes – themes guaranteed to be popular with the contemporary art-buying public – and is known to have painted the occasional society portrait.

Murillo's importance in Seville reached its pinnacle when he helped to set up an Academy of Art – and was appointed its first president. His death in 1682 – after a fall from scaffolding while working on a large commission – did not signal the end of his fame. He has continued to be revered, both in Spain and abroad, during the ensuing centuries.

Ecce Homo, also known as *Suffering Christ*, is a fine example of Murillo's technique of applying delicate brushstrokes to compose his works. He always chose models with empathetic faces for his paintings – as in *Beggar Boys Throwing Dice* (c. 1670), for example – and imbued his compositions with an emotion that retains its significance for the modern-day viewer.

🖎 *Beggar Boys Throwing Dice, The Pie Eater, The Madonna*

Jean Antoine Watteau (1684–1721)

Italian Comedians

National Gallery of Art, Washington. Courtesy of the Bridgeman Art Library

WATTEAU was a key artist of the French Rococo style. In 1702 he moved to Paris, where he discovered an interest in theatrical costume and scenes. While working at the Luxembourg Palace, he admired a series of paintings by Rubens featuring the life of Marie de' Medici. These became the main influence on his style, but he also studied the Venetians, especially Veronese.

He composed his paintings using drawings, often using the same ones over and over. The drawings, in red, white and black, and kept in a bound volume, have survived better than many of his paintings; Watteau lacked sophistication in the technical use of oils.

Watteau excelled as a painter of *fêtes galantes* – charming outdoor scenes – a title created for him in 1717 on his entry into the Academy, and took his subjects from the theatre. Charming though they are, with a fairytale quality, as shown in *Italian Comedians*, his paintings often contain a note of melancholy despite the apparent gaiety. Here an element of loneliness is expressed by the single figure who stands out from the crowd.

He died young, having suffered from tuberculosis for several years, it is suggested that the sadness fundamental to his work may be rooted in his sense of mortality.

The Conversation, The Pilgrimage to the Island of Cythera, The Music Party

William Hogarth (1697–1764)

![Scene from the Beggar's Opera painting]

Scene from the Beggar's Opera
Paul Mellon Collection, USA. Courtesy of the Bridgeman Art Library

HOGARTH trained as an engraver in the Rococo tradition and was an established engraver of bill-heads by 1720. He studied painting at the Academy in St Martin's Lane and by 1729 he was making a name for himself with his 'conversation' pieces – small paintings showing polite social scenes. In 1730 he began to paint portraits, but although gifted, he did not have the flattering temperament of a successful portraitist.

Although he is remembered primarily as an engraver, Hogarth's painting was extremely skilful. He despised the effect of foreign influences on the English, making only occasional forays into painting in the fashionable Italian 'Grand Manner'. These are not considered his best works. This painting, one of the first in

Hogarth's series of satirical scenes, was directed as much at the foibles of society as at its immorality. It portrays the courtroom setting of a contemporary play, *The Beggar's Opera*. Others in the series included melodramas such as *The Rake's Progress* (*c.* 1735) and *Marriage à la Mode* (1743); each resulted in a suitable punishment for their unscrupulous anti-heroes.

He ran an independent academy in St Martin's Lane between 1735 and 1755, which became a forerunner of the Royal Academy, and in 1753 wrote *Analysis of Beauty*.

The Harlot's Progress, The Shrimp Girl, The Roast Beef of Old England (Calais Gate)

ROCOCO

Jean-Baptiste-Siméon Chardin (1699–1779)

House of Cards
Manor House, Stanton Harcourt, Oxon. Courtesy of the Bridgeman Art Library

CHARDIN, a contemporary of Boucher (1703–70), was a painter in the popular bourgeois Dutch realist style. He studied with portrait artist Noel-Nicolas Coypel (1628–1707) and worked on the Grande Galerie at the Palace of Fontainebleau.

As his style was popular and he worked slowly, Chardin often had to copy his paintings to please his buyers. His first wife died in 1735 but he married again in 1744, and produced many portraits of his second wife. He also painted still lifes and in his last years, when he was ill, began to use pastels. Using this faster medium, he produced three masterpieces – *Self-Portrait with Spectacles* (1771), *Self-Portrait with Eyeshade* (1771) and *Madame Chardin* (1775).

Chardin exhibited his paintings for the first time in 1728, and became a member of the Academy in the same year. His still lifes are of simple items – food and kitchen utensils – but they have a depth beyond mere realism. His experiments with impasto and scumbled paint achieved an admirable depth of tone. By the early 1730s he began to paint unsentimental bourgeois genre scenes such as *House of Cards*, using warm but greyish colours. These were very successful when he exhibited them in 1737, and for a time he only painted small domestic scenes.

 The Scullery Maid, Lady Sealing a Letter, Lady with a Bird Organ

The Grand Canal, Venice, Looking East from the Campo di San Vio

Christie's Images. Courtesy of the Bridgeman Art Library

INITIALLY, Canaletto painted scenery for theatres with his father, but after a visit to Rome in 1719, he turned to painting pictures of views. By 1723, his handling of paint exhibited the luminosity and contrast of light and shade that made him famous.

English Consul Joseph Smith promoted Canaletto's work among British travellers to Venice, arranging exhibitions and encouraging the artist to extend his range to include views of Rome and *caprici* – pictures of real buildings set in imaginary scenes. Canaletto also painted pictures of Venice during the festivals and made a series of etchings and drawings, in pen, and pen and wash.

Canaletto made three trips to England, in 1746–50, 1752–53 and 1754–55, but they were not a success. He painted many views of London and country houses but his work became increasingly mannered. He returned to Venice and although he worked until his death, much of his later painting is considered overly mechanical as he used a camera obscura to aid his composition.

The Grand Canal, Venice has all the characteristics of Canaletto's later work, skilfully recording the effects of light and shade on the stonework and water. It depicts his favourite themes; the canals and their teeming life against a backdrop detailed architecture.

Bucintoro at the Molo on Ascension Day, The Stonemason's Yard, A Regatta on the Grand Canal

America (detail)

Wurzburg Residenz, Germany. Courtesy of the Bridgeman Art Library

A VENETIAN, Tiepolo was the greatest decorative Italian painter of the eighteenth century, and the purest of the Italian Rococo artists. He trained under historical painter Gregorio Lazzarini (1655–1730) but his studies of Veronese and contemporary painter Giovanni Battista Piazzetta (1683–1754) had a greater impact on his style.

In 1719 Tiepolo married Cecilia, sister of fellow artists, the Guardi brothers. She bore him nine children. At the time of his marriage, his palette began to lighten and he left behind the dark, sombre tones of Piazzetta and the seventeenth century. By 1725, when he had his first important commission – the fresco decorations at the archbishop's palace in Udine (finished 1728) – his fresh handling, light tones, pale colours and loose style were obvious.

Between 1741–50 Tiepolo was mainly active in Venice. In 1750 he was invited to Würzburg to decorate the Rococo bishop's palace. This figure, representing the continent of America, is part of the allegorical decoration Tiepolo executed here in collaboration with assistants and his sons Giandomenico and Lorenzo.

In 1755 he was elected first President of the Venetian Academy and between 1762–66 decorated the ceilings of the Royal Palace in Madrid. He died suddenly there in 1770 as the Rococo style was giving way to the Neo-Classical movement.

 Danaï, Gathering of the Manna, Antony and Cleopatra

Jean-Honoré Fragonard (1732–1806)

The Prize of a Kiss
Hermitage, St Petersburg. Courtesy of the Bridgeman Art Library

BRIEFLY a pupil of Chardin in 1750, Fragonard studied with Boucher until 1752, when he won the Prix de Rome. He visited Rome in 1756, where he studied the works of Venetian master Tiepolo. On his return to Paris, he made his name with a history painting in the 'Grand Manner', *High Priest Coroesus Sacrificing Himself to Save Callirhoe* (1765). However, once accepted into the Academy, he gave up historical painting and turned to lighter subjects, such as *The Swing* (c. 1766). Although such works often had erotic overtones, they managed to escape accusations of vulgarity through the artist's graceful and lighthearted handling of his subject matter. After his marriage in 1769, Fragonard also painted scenes of family groups.

He worked for the French court of Louis XVI, particularly for his beautiful mistress Mme du Barry. After the Revolution of 1789 and the Terror that followed, Fragonard's patrons disappeared. During this period he fled to Grasse in southern France, returning to Paris in poverty. He was found a job by the Neo-Classical artist Jacques-Louis David (1748–1825) but died in obscurity.

This oil sketch is in keeping with light-hearted, gallant Rococo subject matter, and is painted with a light touch and spontaneity of movement. The colours are soft and bright and there is an element of cheekiness typical of Fragonard.

Progress of Love, Festival at St-Cloud, Boy as Pierrot

Angelica Kauffmann (1741–1807)

Portrait of David Garrick

Burghley House Collection, Lincolnshire. Courtesy of the Bridgeman Art Library

THE daughter of Swiss painter Joseph Johann Kauffmann, Angelica Kauffmann was a child prodigy, executing commissions before the age of 13. She travelled with her father in Austria and Italy, where she copied the art of Correggio and Carracci.

In 1766, Kauffmann visited London and here, under the influence of Sir Joshua Reynolds (1723–92) and Benjamin West (1738–1820), her artistic style began to take on a Neo-Classical flavour. Her portrait style reflected that of Reynolds, with whom there was talk of a clandestine affair. She produced decorative panels for the architect Robert Adam (1728–92) and, although her work is in the Neo-Classical mould, there is a prettiness about it that suggests the Rococo.

Kauffmann made a disastrous first marriage to a bogus Italian count, but was remarried to decorative painter Antonio Zucchi (1726–95) in 1781, when she went to live in Rome. She produced many portraits and decorative paintings but preferred historical painting. Her clients included the royal courts of Naples, Russia and Austria. Often dismissed as a decorative painter, she achieved financial success and was a founder member of the Royal Academy in London. This portrait of actor and theatre manager David Garrick (1717–79), skilfully captures of the personality of the sitter.

 *Cornelia Pointing to her Children as her Treasures, Johann Joachim Winckelmann, Cupid's Wound*

ROCOCO

François Boucher (1703–70)

Woman at Her Toilette

Agnew and Sons, London. Courtesy of the Bridgeman Art Library

BOUCHER was a leading exponent of Rococo decorative art, painting charming and often salacious mythological and pastoral scenes, although he also painted portraits, designs for tapestries, ceiling decorations and accessories such as fans and shoes. His style was influenced by the works of Veronese, Rubens and Watteau.

He began his career as an engraver of Watteau's works, winning the Prix de Rome in 1721. He travelled to Rome in 1727 before returning to Paris in 1731, where he became a fashionable artist – his work epitomised the elegance and frivolity of contemporary French court life. His most discerning patron was Madame de Pompadour, the elegant mistress of Louis XV, whom he taught to draw and painted several times. He became the director of the Gobelins tapestry factory in 1755, Director of the Academy and King's Painter in 1765.

This roundel, part of a decorative scheme, is an unusual example of Boucher's work in that it shows a single figure against a sombre background. As she sits at the dressing table, the woman looks at a miniature portrait of her beloved. Her skin shows the high colouring and porcelain quality typical of Boucher at his best. In his old age, he gave up using models, complaining that nature was 'too green and ill-lit'.

Rinaldo and Armida, Young Girl Resting, Mme de Pompadour

Johann Zoffany (1733–1810)

Charles Towneley's Library in Park Street

Towneley Hall Art Gallery and Museum, Burnley. Courtesy of the Bridgeman Art Library

JOHANN ZOFFANY was born and educated in Germany. Like many artists before him, he travelled to Italy to study the classical and Renaissance masters. In Rome, Zoffany studied under fellow German, Anton Mengs (1728–79). By 1760 Zoffany had moved to London, where he became one of the founding members of the Royal Academy. He quickly gained popularity among the elite of London society, with a client list that included included King George III and other members of the royal family. As well as society portraits Zoffany produced theatre decorations and several 'conversation pieces'. Conversation pieces – group portraits that show the sitters occupied in an activity – were a popular subject for painting in the eighteenth century. Several of his conversation pieces depict groups of cultured men surrrounded by art, and *Charles Towneley's Library in Park Street* is a good example.

Towneley and Zoffany met in Florence, where they became firm friends. Here, Towneley is seen in profile, with his dog by his feet. The room is filled with classical sculptures, friezes and busts. The men in the group are shown studying books or conversing. Zoffany succeeds in portraying the men as the intellectual, rational leaders of their society, while at the same time showing off their excellent taste and obvious wealth.

 Queen Charlotte with the Prince of Wales and Duke of York, Cognoscenti in the Uffizi, The Life School at the Royal Academy

Jacques-Louis David (1748–1825)

Death of Marat
Royal Beaux-Arts Museum of Belgium, Brussels. Courtesy of the Bridgeman Art Library

JACQUES-LOUIS DAVID was a leading figure in the French Revolution, as well as the foremost French Neo-Classical painter. A student of Boucher (1703–70) and the teacher of Ingres (1780–1867), David became an integral part of the French art establishment.

David was a fervent supporter of Napoleon (1769–1821), whom he depicted on several canvases, and was among the influential citizens of France who passed judgement on Louis XVI, calling for his execution.

Jean-Paul Marat was a leader of the French Revolution of 1789, and a personal friend of David. Marat became a martyr to the cause when he was stabbed to death in his bath by Charlotte Corday, a fervent royalist. The letter the dead man holds in his hand was her faked letter of introduction, with which she had fraudulently entered his home.

This portrait of Marat encapsulates the artist's grief, political fervour and artistic ability. *Death of Marat* was a personal homage to David's friend, as seen by the inscription on the side of the makeshift desk, as well as an historic record. The portrayal, particularly fine in the brushwork re-creating the corpse, is a technique that can be seen in the work of Ingres (1780–1867).

 Napoleon Crossing the Alps, The Death of Socrates, Madame Récamier

NEO-CLASSICAL

Sir Henry Raeburn (1756–1823)

The Reverend Robert Walker Skating
National Gallery of Scotland, Edinburgh. Courtesy of the Bridgeman Art Library

HENRY RAEBURN was born near Edinburgh and began his career painting miniatures, a skill which he taught himself. In about 1776 Raeburn switched to painting portraits and became the leading Scottish portrait painter of his generation. Following his advantageous marriage in 1778, Raeburn became financially secure, enabling him to travel. In 1785, after visiting Sir Joshua Reynolds (1723–1792) in London, he travelled to Italy where he studied in Rome for several years. However, the years spent abroad did not have a profound effect on Raeburn's style.

Returning in 1787, Raeburn settled in Edinburgh, and very quickly became a highly prolific portrait artist. It is estimated that Raeburn produced about one thousand portraits of the key people in Scottish society. In 1792 an exhibition of works by Raeburn was held in the Royal Academy, and in 1815 he was elected as a Royal Academician. Henry Raeburn received his knighthood from King George VI in 1822.

This unusual and charming portrait of *The Reverend Robert Walker Skating* is Raeburn's most famous image. The pose of the vicar in mid-flight as he skates across the frozen lake is at once dramatic and comic. The darkly dressed figure is set against a vibrant but vaguely defined landscape, as if seen at dusk.

 Portrait of Sir John Sinclair, Robert Dundas, Mrs James Cruikshank

Lavinia Bingham, Second Countess Spencer
Collection of Earl Spencer, Althorp, Nottinghamshire. Courtesy of the Bridgeman Art Library

DURING his lifetime, Sir Joshua Reynolds was considered the finest portrait painter in England. Born in Plympton, Devon, he was apprenticed to Thomas Hudson (1701–79) and had his own workshop by the age of 20. In 1749 his former master sponsored a trip to Italy, where he studied classical sculpture and the Renaissance masters. As a consequence, Reynolds' aim was to elevate art once again to the level of the Italian Renaissance masters; he assiduously copied their style of painting, emulating their brushwork and using similar poses and iconography, in an attempt to simulate their grandeur. Reynolds' importance in art history is underlined by his academic achievements. He was the first president of the Royal Academy, which opened in 1768. He delivered 15 discourses on art to students there, and his opinions were respected by several generations of artists. By 1789, having lost his sight in one eye, Reynolds stopped painting.

Reynolds' portraits brought him widespread popularity and fame, although he himself preferred the genre of historical painting. His beliefs that only aristocratic and elite members of society made suitable portrait subjects, and that art should be refined in both style and content, is encapsulated in this portrait of Lavinia Bingham, Second Countess Spencer.

Lady Caroline Howard, Joseph Baretti, The Countess Spencer with her Daughter Georgiana

NEO-CLASSICAL

Jean-Auguste-Dominique Ingres (1780–1867)

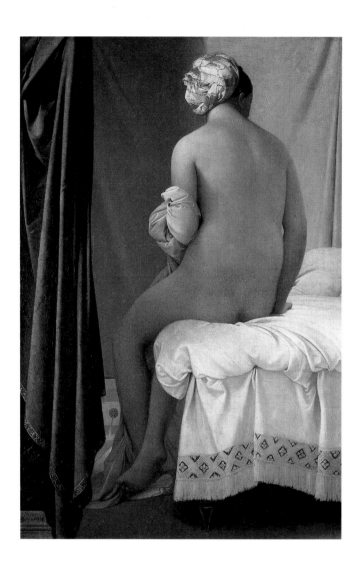

The Bather
Louvre, Paris. Courtesy of the Bridgeman Art Library

INGRES was sent to the Toulouse Academy at the age of 11 by his artist father. From there he went to Paris in 1797 to study with Jacques-Louis David (1748–1825). In 1801 he won the Prix de Rome, and went there in 1807. He stayed for 18 years, receiving little acclaim in Paris.

Ingres earned his living by painting and drawing portraits, although he also produced historical paintings. He was a skilled draughtsman, noted for his sinuous line and expressive contour. However, although technically without reproach, he often distorted shapes, elongating them in the manner of Botticelli and Raphael, whom he venerated. *La Grande Odalisque* (1814), one of several nudes painted in Rome, was criticised for having such a long back.

When Ingres returned to Paris in 1824, he became a leading figure of French Neo-Classicism. Following his success, he spent much of his time working on two large works, including *The Apotheosis of Homer*, a ceiling painting for the Louvre, which was installed in 1827. He continued working into his 80s.

The superb draughtsmanship and clarity of shapes, light and line in *The Bather* are typical of Ingres' graceful nudes. Such works had a strong influence on Degas, whose many nude studies echo the scene shown here.

 The Ambassadors of Agamemnon, Portrait of Mme Moitessier, La Grande Odalisque

Antonio Canova (1757–1822)

The Three Graces

Belvoir Castle, Leicestershire. Courtesy of the Bridgeman Art Library

ANTONIO CANOVA was arguably the greatest sculptor of his time. His ability to turn marble into a likeness of living, supple flesh remains breathtaking to this day. In his own time his influence was such that, almost single-handedly, he turned the accepted fashion in sculpture from Baroque to Neo-Classical. His ability to recreate the female form with sensuous accuracy is evident in a late work, *A Sleeping Nymph* (1820–22).

The son of a stonemason, Canova was born in Possagno, Italy, and worked as a sculptor from childhood. He left home at the age of 13, accompanying his sculpting master to Venice; he remained there until 1781, when he moved to Rome. Here, he became a great favourite of society, including the pope, who bestowed upon him the title Marchese d'Ischia. He had earned the honour by travelling to France to reclaim Italian works of art stolen by Napoleon's troops – he so impressed Napoleon by his courage that the leader attempted to persuade Canova to stay.

The Three Graces, admired for its purity of line and anatomical clarity, is one of Canova's best-known works. The sensuous curves and Canova's striving for symmetry in the design can be divined in this ensemble, and is also clearly evident in his masterful *Cupid and Psyche* (1793).

Tomb of Pope Clement XIV, Tomb of Archduchess Maris Christina, Pauline Bonaparte Borghese as Venus

Neo-Classical

Centaur in the Village Blacksmith's Shop

Museum of Fine Arts, Budapest. Courtesy of the Bridgeman Art Library

NEO-CLASSICAL

ARNOLD Böcklin was a Swiss artist who lived in Italy for much of his life. His passion for the mythology of both ancient Greece and Rome (seen in the centaur shown here), as well as that of less well-known Swiss and German folklore, is evident in much of his work.

Böcklin's early style focused on idealised classical landscapes, but in the 1870s he began to illustrate grotesque, distorted images from German legends, possibly in response to operatic works such as the *Ring Cycle* by Richard Wagner (1813–83). Later his work became identified with the Symbolist movement. Some of his more unusual compositions, such as *Centaur's Combat* (1873), with its grotesquely twisted forms and dream-like background images, inspired artists of the Surrealist school.

In *Centaur in the Village Blacksmith's Shop* there is a marked difference between Böcklin's representation of the centaur and that of the roughly painted beasts in *Centaur's Combat*, painted 15 years earlier. In this later work, Böcklin's mythological beast is depicted as an amiable presence – in sharp contrast with the bare-chested, bare-legged blacksmith and the peasant women with their baby. Böcklin presents the human figures in such a way that they appear insubstantial, whereas the centaur appears corporeal.

 Pan in the Reeds, The Island of the Dead, Triton and Nereid

Thomas Gainsborough (1727–88)

Mr and Mrs Andrews
The National Gallery, London. Courtesy of the Bridgeman Art Gallery

GAINSBOROUGH was born in Sudbury, Suffolk. He was, at heart, a landscape painter, although he painted portraits for a living. He went to London in around 1740, where he studied as an engraver with Hubert-François Gravelot (1699–1773), who had been a pupil of Rococo artist Antoine Watteau. In 1759 he moved to Bath and painted society portraits, developing an elegant, glamorous style inspired by Van Dyck. He painted full-length female portraits and was noted for his exact likenesses, something his rival Sir Joshua Reynolds (1723–92) was said to find detrimental to the grandeur of his own paintings.

In 1768 Gainsborough was elected as an Academician at the Royal Academy in London and four years later he moved to the capital. His style developed into light brushstrokes and delicate colours. From the 1780s he painted genre pictures of peasants in a style after Murillo (1618–82), as an extension of his interest in landscape. He painted and drew landscapes throughout his life.

Mr and Mrs Andrews, painted while Gainsborough was still in Sudbury, is notable for its innocence in comparison with late work, with the couple being moved to one side so that the landscape can be seen properly. When Gainsborough died, Reynolds paid tribute him in his 14th Discourse at the Royal Academy.

Ann Ford, The Blue Boy, The Morning Walk (Mr and Mrs Hallett)

NEO-CLASSICAL

Henry Fuseli (1741–1825)

The Nightmare

Goethe Museum, Frankfurt. Courtesy of the Bridgeman Art Library

HENRY FUSELI was born in Switzerland, the son of a painter and writer, Johann Caspar Fuseli (sometimes spelt Füssli, 1707–82). His father's love of art and literature was transmitted to his son, manifesting itself in such works as *The Death of Oedipus* (1784) and *Titania and Bottom* (c. 1780–90), as well as in Henry's later career as an art critic.

At the age of 20, Henry Fuseli was ordained as a pastor, but a disagreement with his father prompted him to leave Switzerland and the church. He travelled throughout Europe, studying in Germany and Italy, where he was influenced by Michelangelo (1475–1564), before arriving in London. He was soon accepted into the London art-world and became a member of the Royal Academy in 1790. Despite frequent visits to Europe, including to his native Switzerland, he always returned to London.

Fuseli's enigmatic, dreamlike *Nightmare* was exhibited at the Royal Academy in 1790, bringing him wide public acclaim and instant fame. The unsettling subject matter and treatment reveal the disparate influences of Classicism (engendered by his study of Michelangelo), the grotesque, as seen in the work of Arcimboldo, and the work of William Blake (1757–1827).

 The Death of Oedipus, Titania and Bottom, The Artist in Despair over the Magnitude of Antique Fragments

George Stubbs (1724–1806)

Mambrino

Private Collection. Courtesy of the Bridgeman Art Library

GEORGE STUBBS was born in Liverpool in 1724. Although his art education was informal and short, he showed a flair for portraiture. He used this skill to support himself during time spent studying anatomy in York. In 1756, on his return to England after travelling in Italy, George Stubbs led an isolated existence while he devoted himself to further anatomical study, which was now exclusively of horses. Stubbs moved to London in 1760, where his lifelike paintings of sporting and racing events found a large audience. The year 1766 saw the publication of his *Anatomy of the Horse*. He died leaving a further, unpublished, text on the comparative anatomy of humans, tigers and common fowl. Stubbs's accomplished paintings of horses brought him many aristocratic patrons. This painting of *Mambrino* is one of several studies by Stubbs of the favoured horse. His skill at depicting a horse's form came from his carefully gained anatomical knowledge. For each painting, Stubbs made in-depth studies of musculature and movement before beginning to work. Stubbs's paintings reveal a high level of 'finish' as well as painstaking attention to detail.

Although Stubbs is remembered now for his reverential paintings of horses, he produced paintings of various other animals, as well as portraits and conversation pieces.

Mares and Foals in a Landscape, A Horse Frightened by a Lion, Returning from the Hunt

ROMANTIC

William Blake (1757–1827)

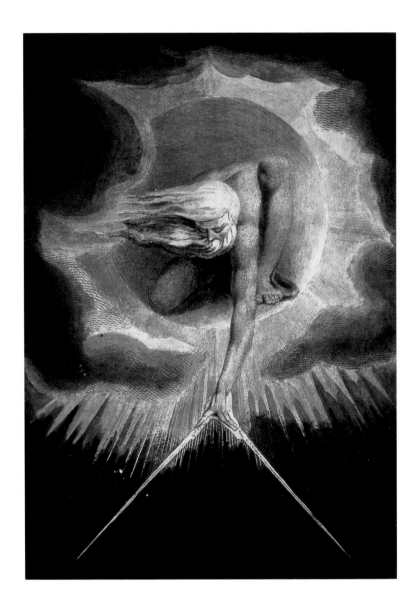

The Ancient of Days
British Museum, London. Courtesy of the Bridgeman Art Library

WILLIAM BLAKE was born in London. His figure drawing was learned by copying plaster casts of ancient statues under the tutelage of Henry Pars (*c.* 1733–1806). He trained briefly at London's Royal Academy, although he did not agree with the principles of the school or the teachings of Sir Joshua Reynolds. He still continued to exhibit at the Academy throughout his life.

Blake was a visionary, a poet and artist who strove for social and political freedom for all. His works ranged from the religious, such as *The Ancient of Days* to the grotesque, such as *Ghost of a Flea* (1819–20). Along with his contemporary, the Spanish painter and etcher Goya (1746–1828), Blake rebelled against the accepted teachings of the contemporary art world, disrupting eighteenth-

century art with his terrifying emotions and radical perspectives. Blake's writings included two collections of poems, called *Songs of Innocence* (1789) and *Songs of Experience* (1794), the famous hymn 'Jerusalem', and, at his death, was partway through illustrating the works of Dante Alighieri (1265–1321).

The Ancient of Days is an etching, engraved into metal and coloured by hand. It harks back to medieval days, with its belief in God as the architect of the world. It is evocative of another of Blake's works, *Newton* (1795).

 Group of Negroes, as Imported to be Sold for Slaves, Whirlwind of Lovers, Angels Watching Over the Tomb of Christ

John Martin (1789–1854)

Sadak in Search of the Waters of Oblivion

Southampton City Art Gallery, Hampshire. Courtesy of the Bridgeman Art Library

WITH the emergence of the Romantic movement in the eighteenth century, art turned towards the splendour of nature and man's spiritual relationship with it. John Martin was one of the major exponents of Romantic painting. Born in Northumberland, he began his career as an enamel painter. Martin's volume of work is relatively small – his career was cut short when he suffered a stroke. He painted several biblical stories but, rather than focusing on the human narrative, he chose to show stormy, dramatic landscapes that evoke intensely turbulent emotions. In common with other Romantic painters, Martin took inspiration from the literary works of poets Lord Byron (1788–1824) and John Milton (1608–74), as well as from Nordic myths. He did not paint realistic landscapes. Instead, his painting sprang from an internal vision, earning him the nickname 'Mad Martin'.

Many of his paintings have an overwhelming physical presence. He used large canvases, filling them with passionate scenes which intimidated the viewer. *Sadak in Search of the Waters of Oblivion*, as in many of his works, includes tiny figures set in the foreground against a domineering landscape. This technique emphasises the insignificance of man when compared to the solidity of nature, as personified by the devastating force of a storm.

The Great Day of His Wrath, Joshua Commanding the Sun to Stand Still, The Flood

ROMANTIC

Francisco Goya
y Lucientes (1746–1828)

Execution of the Defenders of Madrid, 3rd May 1808

Prado, Madrid. Courtesy of the Bridgeman Art Library

SPANISH painter Goya spent his early career in Saragossa and moved to Madrid in 1863. Here he was trained by Francisco Bayeu y Subías (1734–95), whose sister he married in 1773. Between 1775–92, he designed tapestries in the Rococo style and painted portraits and religious scenes.

In 1792, Goya suffered an unknown illness that left him deaf. He became introspective and obsessed with the morbid and bizarre themes that haunted his later work. He also found fame with his portraits, becoming court painter to Charles IV in 1799.

In 1808 Spain was invaded by France and Joseph Bonaparte was placed on the Spanish throne. Goya was sickened by the barbarity of the French soldiers, executing this painting in response to a

bloody incident in May 1808 when their troops murdered Spanish civilians. This is one of his most forceful and emotive works – the pathos of the condemned man's gesture, illuminated in a white shirt by the lantern light, is intensely moving.

In 1820, after a second serious illness, he painted 14 murals, known as his 'Black Paintings', showing dark, horrific scenes that were painted in a free, almost Impressionistic manner. In 1824 he was exiled to France and was employed as a portrait painter by the Bourbon French Royal family.

 Portrait of Charles IV and his Family, Clothed Maja, Naked Maja

Sir Thomas Lawrence (1769–1830)

The Duke of Wellington
Private Collection. Courtesy of the Bridgeman Art Library

ENGLISH portrait painter Sir Thomas Lawrence was one of the most talented artists of his time. Almost entirely self-taught, he studied at the Royal Academy in London in 1786–87, and was accepted as an Academician in 1791. His first full-length portrait, *Lady Cremone* (1789), led to his portrait of Queen Charlotte, which he exhibited in 1791 to great acclaim. He succeeded Sir Joshua Reynolds in 1792 as painter to King George III.

By 1806 he had consolidated his talent, and half-length portraits of men replaced the stylish full-length female portraits of his earlier period. He was knighted in 1815 and sent to Europe as an envoy of the Prince Regent (the future George IV) in 1818 to paint the heads of state and military leaders (including Wellington, shown here) who had been involved in the defeat of Napoleon. He visited Venice and Rome in 1818, where he painted the Pope, Pius VII, and was appointed President of the Royal Academy in London in 1820. His portrait style emulated that of Reynolds, but had a fashionable note of modernity and theatricality – he often lowered the horizon, for example, as in *The Duke of Wellington*, to silhouette his figures sharply against the sky. His fluid and lush brushwork won the admiration of Romantic French painters such as Delacroix (1798–1863), who painted portraits in his style.

Miss Farren, Elizabeth, Lady Conyngham as Diana the Huntress, The Archduke of Austria

ROMANTIC

Grey Dapple Horse

Christie's Images, London. Courtesy of the Bridgeman Art Library

GÉRICAULT'S career lasted for only a decade; for someone with such a small body of work, he had a huge impact. He studied in Paris with both Carle Vernet (1758–1836) and Pierre Guérin (1774–1833), but he was influenced more by the Old Masters, especially Rubens (1577–1640). His subject matter – horses and contemporary subjects – shows the influence of the painter Antoine-Jean Gros (1771–1835), Napoleon's official war painter.

Géricault visited Italy in 1816–18, and on his return to Paris, he exhibited *The Raft of the Medusa* (1819). Although it received the gold medal at the Salon, it still caused a political scandal because its subject matter appeared to imply criticism of the government. The epic treatment of a contemporary event was also innovative.

Between 1820–22 Géricault visited England, during which time he painted jockeys and racecourses and made lithographs showing the poverty that was rife on the streets of London. From 1822–23 he painted ten portraits of patients at La Salpetrière, the lunatic asylum in Paris. The spontaneous brushwork of *Grey Dapple Horse* and the drama of the pose and lighting are typical of Géricault's Romantic style. The influence on the young contemporary artist, Delacroix (1798–1863) is easy to see.

Géricault died tragically early after falling from a horse.

 Light Cavalry Officer Charging, The Raft of the Medusa, Epsom Derby

The Haywain

The National Gallery, London. Courtesy of the Bridgeman Art Library

CONSTABLE was born in Suffolk, the son of a wealthy industrialist; he lived there until 1795, when he moved to London. Although he received some early training, Constable was largely self-taught until 1799, when he entered the Royal Academy. The countryside was to remain an inspiration to him throughout his life – he was fascinated by the effects of light and by cloud formations.

Although he was influenced by Claude Lorrain (1600–82) and Poussin (1594–1665), Constable preferred to learn his art from nature, rather than from other artists' interpretation of it. He was averse to studio work, preferring to paint out of doors.

In middle age Constable suffered from severe depression, and this is reflected in the brooding light, dark, lowering clouds and gloomy atmosphere of many of his later works, such as *The Valley Farm* (1835) and *Stoke-by-Nayland* (1836–37). Here, the brushwork is less distinct – almost Impressionistic – in contrast with the clarity of his earlier paintings, such as *The Haywain*.

The Haywain was painted on a visit to his native Stour Valley, an area to which he often returned. The colours of the sky, the water and the dappled light on the field are indicative of the many hours Constable spent sketching nature to perfect his technique.

Dedham Lock and Mill, The White Horse, Salisbury Cathedral from the Bishop's Garden

ROMANTIC

Eugène Delacroix (1798–1863)

Massacre at Chios
Louvre, Paris. Courtesy of the Bridgeman Art Library

DELACROIX began his career as a musician, and his decision to become an artist was aided by his friend and teacher Géricault (1791–1824). It may be no coincidence that this emotive picture was painted in the year of Géricault's death. Alongside Géricault, Delacroix became a leading figure of the nineteenth-century Romantic movement in French art. There was a constant rivalry between Delacroix and the other, more conventional, leading painter of the day, Ingres (1780–1867). Delacroix travelled to England in 1825, where he greatly admired the work of English painter, John Constable (1776–1837). After seeing Constable's work at the Royal Academy in London, Delacroix returned to the already finished *Massacre at Chios* and reworked it. A visit to

North Africa in 1832 inspired the exotic subject matter of much of Delacriox's later work, such as *Women of Algiers* (1834). *Massacre at Chios* relates an incident from the Greco-Turkish War in 1824. As the Greeks struggled to liberate themselves from Turkish occupation, over 20,000 soldiers were slaughtered by their oppressors. In the painting, Delacroix emphasises the Turks' brutality by his impassivity; his face looks down, without emotion, at the carnage beneath him. Delacroix was sympathetic to the Greeks' cause, but his journal records that he chose the subject matter for its topicality, assuring maximum publicity for his work.

 Liberty Leading the People, Death of Sardanapalus, Women of Algiers

Wreck of the Hope or The Arctic Shipwreck
Kunsthalle, Hamburg. Courtesy of the Bridgeman Art Library

CASPAR DAVID FRIEDRICH was one of the foremost German Romantic landscape painters. He attended Copenhagen Academy (1794–8) but was largely self-taught. He moved to Dresden in 1798, where he moved in Romantic literary circles, and remained there for most of his life. Initially he was a topographical artist, working in pencil and wash. He took up oil painting in 1807, and his first commission, *Cross on the Mountain* (1808), an altarpiece for a private chapel, caused controversy because the spirituality of his landscape was considered sacrilegious.

His introspective and melancholic subjects, which included cemeteries in the snow, fog-bound landscapes and seashores at dusk, were often ground-breaking. He suffered a stroke in 1835 and thereafter returned to working in sepia. His work was virtually forgotten until its rediscovery by artists of the Symbolist movement.

In *Wreck of the Hope*, Friedrich's technique is polished and precise, and strongly suggestive of a 'tragedy of nature', as one contemporary put it. He was especially interested in light and the effects of the seasons. Here, the light on the ice creates a searing purity, conjuring up the extreme cold and also highlighting the tragedy in the aftermath of a drama.

 Procession at Dawn, Woman in the Morning Sun, The Large Enclosure

Thomas Cole (1801–48)

Scene from The Last of the Mohicans

New York Historical Society. Courtesy of the Bridgeman Art Library

COLE lived in England until the age of 17, when his family, who were part American, part English, moved to Ohio in the US. He had begun his artistic training in England and was able to continue his studies at the Philadelphia Academy of Art. In later years he helped found and was considered the leader of the Hudson River School, a group of artists who shared a love of the emptiness and monumentality of the American landscape and strove to capture its grandeur on canvas. They worked mainly around the Hudson River and the nearby Catskill Mountains and paid great attention to the showing of nature in its overwhelming detail. Cole was also instrumental in establishing the Romantic movement within the US art world.

In order to improve his style, Cole travelled through Europe. His desire was to study the works of the great landscape masters, in particular Poussin (1594–1665) and Claude Lorrain (1600–82), and to experience for himself the lands that had inspired them.

This painting, inspired by the book *The Last of the Mohicans* by James Fenimore Cooper (1789–1851), is typical of Cole's work – not only for its subject matter, in which the rugged landscape, reaching far into the distance, assumes obvious mastery over the figures, but also for its wealth of detail.

 The Giant's Chalice, The Voyage of Life, The Course of Empire

William Etty (1787–1849)

Hero and Leander

York City Art Gallery, North Yorkshire. Courtesy of the Bridgeman Art Library

WILLIAM ETTY was one of the few British painters to paint nudes, for which he was viewed with suspicion. He was born in York but studied and worked in London, training at the Royal Academy and then with Sir Thomas Lawrence (1769–1830), whose influence intially included a warm use of colour which was later modified by Etty's trips to Italy.

He visited Europe several times and studied artists such as Pierre-Narcisse Guérin (1774–1833), Titian and Van Dyck – all highly skilled colourists. He met French Romantic painter Delacroix in 1828. The work of Rubens was influential in creating the sensual, glowing style that Etty primarily applied to his nude female studies; as a result, his work was often considered lush and indecent.

Etty's paintings show faithful studies of nudes, presented as mythological or historical characters, as here in the story of the Greek lovers Hero and Leander. Hero swims the raging seas each night to be with his lover but one fateful night he drowns. Leander, on discovering his lifeless body, commits suicide.

Etty studied life drawing at the Royal Academy throughout his life. His drawings are now his most admired works – many of his paintings seem vapid by comparison. He lived in poverty, only achieving fame shortly before his death.

Cleopatra's Arrival in Cilicia, Youth on the Prow and Pleasure on the Helm, Venus and her Satellites

ROMANTIC

Joseph Mallord
William Turner (1775–1851)

Venice
Victoria and Albert Museum. Courtesy of the Bridgeman Art Library

A KEY figure of the Romantic movement, Turner is also popularly viewed as the greatest English landscape painter. Born in London, the son of a baker, Turner refused to hide his humble background and retained both his Cockney accent and manners, despite his aristocratic friends and patronage. He received his initial training from an architectural topographer before entering the Royal Academy in 1789, where he exhibited at the precocious age of 15. In 1791 he toured North Wales and Scotland before travelling to Switzerland, making sketches and watercolours of landscapes. Although his range increased in later years, Turner's main subjects were land or seascapes, and historical narratives. By the middle of his career he focussed on an emotive, instinctual representation of light and the drama of extreme weather. The accurate portrayal in painting of the effect of light at different times of day became more important to him than recording a representation of the true facts. Turner's late paintings are blurred, with whirls of seeping colours. In this respect, they anticipate the loose brushwork of the Impressionist movement, especially Claude Monet (1840–1926).

After 1819 Turner made several other tours, visiting Italy repeatedly. The city of Venice made a lasting and deep impression on him. This painting is one of his many illustrations of the city.

Hannibal Crossing the Alps, Rain, Steam and Speed

George Bingham (1811–79)

Ferrymen Playing Cards
St Louis Art Museum, Missouri. Courtesy of the Bridgeman Art Library

GEORGE CALEB BINGHAM was born in the American county of Augusta, Virginia, but lived for most of his life in Kansas City, Missouri. Before the widespread use of photography, his work was vitally important as a faithful record of the realities of life in contemporary Frontier America.

Bingham was remarkable, chiefly, for two reasons: he was almost entirely self-taught; and he managed to combine his artistic career with one in politics as an elected member of the Missouri state government. The periods of Bingham's life in which he underwent formal artistic training were a few months which were spent at the Pennsylvania Academy of Fine Arts, and during a short stay in Düsseldorf, Germany, in the 1850s. His skill was honed by

travelling throughout Europe, where he studied the art of other cultures and eras, and by time spent in reflection on the magnificent landscapes of the Mid-west.

In addition to his concern with composition and use of colour, his paintings are evocative of a time long past, when America was wild and sparsely populated. In *Ferrymen Playing Cards*, the still waters provide a calming background to a moment caught in time – the same effect was used in an earlier masterpiece, *Fur Traders Descending the Missouri* (1845).

Fur Traders Descending the Missouri, Jolly Flatboatmen, County Election

Sir Edwin Landseer (1802–73)

The Monarch of the Glen

United Distillers and Vintners, Edinburgh. Courtesy of the Bridgeman Art Library

EDWIN LANDSEER was a successful English painter, sculptor and engraver who specialised in the depiction of animals. The son of John Landseer, an engraver and writer, Edwin was an infant prodigy, exhibiting at the Royal Academy aged 12, and becoming an Academician at 24. He refused the presidency in 1865.

The excellent draughtsmanship and fluid technique of Landseer's early career gave way to sentimental genre scenes of animals which were meant to imply the natural morality of the animal kingdom. These mawkish images were highly prized in Victorian England and became widely known through engravings, many done by Landseer's brother, Thomas (1798–1880). Landseer led a socially and professionally successful life, and was a favourite of Queen Victoria and was friendly with the novelists Charles Dickens (1812–70) and William Thackeray (1811–63). He visited Scotland regularly and *The Monarch of the Glen* is one of the least sentimental of many paintings inspired by his visits, although the idea of a king surveying his domain is implicit in the grandeur of the animal, which is lit from behind by the glowing mist. It was painted the same year that Landseer received a knighthood. He became mentally ill in 1869 and died four years later. He was buried in St Paul's Cathedral.

 The Old Shepherd's Chief Mourner, Wild Cattle at Chillingham, Dignity and Impudence

The Last of England
Birmingham Museum and Art Gallery. Courtesy of the Bridgeman Art Library

FORD MADOX BROWN was born in France of English parents. His artistic training took place in the Low Countries, before he moved to England in 1844. His continental education, and an indebtedness to eighteenth-century Dutch and Flemish painters, is evident in works such as *The Pretty Baa Lambs* (1852). Although Brown was not strictly part of the Pre-Raphaelite Brotherhood, he knew the group well through his role as Dante Gabriel Rossetti's (1828–82) art tutor, and remained inextricably associated with them throughout his life. He was instrumental in encouraging Elizabeth Siddal (1829–62), Rossetti's wife, in her artistic career.

Brown was seldom satisfied with his pictures, often returning to rework them. He constantly absorbed influences from those around him, and his later works, including stained glass, owe much to the rich colours used by Rossetti. Brown's own political ideology also had a strong influence on his art, notably on the superb oil painting, *Work* (1868).

The watercolour *The Last of England* was based on the actual emigration to Australia of Thomas Woolner (1825–92), one of the Pre-Raphaelite Brotherhood. Like the Pre-Raphaelites, Brown used his family and friends as models – the models here are Brown himself and his wife, Emma.

 Work, Take Your Son, Sir, Chaucer at the Court of Edward III

PRE-RAPHAELITE

Sir John Everett Millais (1829–96)

Sir Isumbras at the Ford (detail)
Lady Lever Art Gallery, Port Sunlight, Merseyside. Courtesy of the Bridgeman Art Library

JOHN EVERETT MILLAIS was born in Jersey. Recognising his prodigious artistic talent, his parents moved to London to allow him to study at the Royal Academy. He was a universal favourite with both tutors and students, although his association with the Pre-Raphaelite Brotherhood (of which he was a founder member) caused the senior Academicians great alarm.

Early works, such as the exquisite *Lorenzo and Isabella* (1849) and his powerful portrait of John Ruskin (1853), prove the magnificence of Millais' artistic ability. In 1852, he exhibited *The Huguenot*, the overwhelming success of which projected Millais to the forefront of society at a time when the Pre-Raphaelite Brotherhood was in demise. He began painting much-coveted society portraits, as well as sentimental scenes that would appeal to Victorian art buyers.

Sir Isumbras at the Ford was executed with this market in mind, although it is also indicative of Millais' prodigious ability as a portraitist. Unfortunately, later paintings such as *Bubbles* (1886) and *The Boyhood of Raleigh* (1870) have led to Millais being associated, in the twentieth-century mind, with sickly-sweet Victorian sentimentality.

 Ophelia, Lorenzo and Isabella, The Black Brunswicker

Frederic, Lord Leighton (1830–96)

Nausicaa

Christie's Images, London. Courtesy of the Bridgeman Art Library

LORD LEIGHTON was a British artist and sculptor who is usually associated with Sir Lawrence Alma-Tadema (1836–1912) as an exponent of High Victorian Art. He grew up in continental Europe, although he moved to London in 1860.

Leighton was not a member of the Pre-Raphaelite Brotherhood, although many of his beliefs and methods were identical to theirs – his fidelity to natural light and his use of subjects from literature and mythology, for example. Leighton's predeliction for nudes and semi-clad women led to many of his paintings being removed from a late-nineteenth-century exhibition of English art that toured America. His sculpted figure, *Athlete Wrestling with a Python* (1877), encapsulates Leighton's return to the Classical ideals of antiquity.

The subject of *Nausicaa* is from Homer's *Odyssey*. According to legend, Nausicaa was a princess who found Odysseus washed up after a shipwreck. Here she looks wistful; one imagines her eyes straying in the direction of Odysseus. The provocatively transparent material of her dress is typical of Leighton; a similar effect can be seen in his famous *Flaming June* (1895). Also typical are the skilfully rendered marble column against which Nausicaa leans, and the beauty of the model's face.

Lieder ohne Worte, The Bath of Psyche, Flaming June

William Holman Hunt (1827–1910)

Isabella and the Pot of Basil

Laing Art Gallery, Newcastle-upon-Tyne. Courtesy of the Bridgeman Art Library

WILLIAM HOLMAN HUNT was a forceful member of the Pre-Raphaelite Brotherhood. An early mentor of Rossetti (1828–82), Hunt later quarrelled with his former friend about personal and professional matters – Rossetti had an affair with Hunt's first fiancée, and both men claimed to have been the guiding force behind the Pre-Raphaelite Brotherhood. Hunt was a great admirer of John Ruskin (1819–1900), and the only one of the seven members of the Pre-Raphaelite Brotherhood to adhere to its principles throughout his career – he chose religious and literary themes for his works and was a strong exponent of painting in natural light, rather than executing his work in the studio. When creating *The Light of the World* (1853) he spent several months painting by moonlight in his garden, earning himself a reputation locally as a madman. Hunt spent much of his life travelling, particularly in Europe and the Middle East, where he was inspired by the vibrant colours and clear light, as well as the local materials and architecture. *Isabella and the Pot of Basil*, based on a poem by John Keats (1795–1821), was painted in Italy. The model was Hunt's heavily pregnant wife, Fanny, who modelled tirelessly until their son was born but died shortly afterwards. Hunt later married Fanny's younger sister, Edith, which caused a scandal in British society, contributing to Hunt's continual travelling.

 The Lady of Shalott, The Scapegoat, The Light of the World

Sir Edward Coley Burne-Jones (1833–98)

The Heart Desires

Birmingham Museum and Art Gallery, Birmingham. Courtesy of the Bridgeman Art Library

BURNE-JONES and William Morris (1834–96), although not members of the Pre-Raphaelite Brotherhood, were extremely important to the Pre-Raphaelite movement. They are generally considered as the second generation of Pre-Raphaelites. Burne-Jones was a pupil of Rossetti (1828–82) and remained in awe of the older artist throughout his life. Much of his early work is almost indistinguishable from that of his teacher. However, Burne-Jones's output evolved gradually over the years and, by the end of his life, his work was defined entirely by his own individual style. His later work moved away from the Pre-Raphaelite mould and towards the burgeoning Art Nouveau movement. In common with other Pre-Raphaelites, Burne-Jones took much of his inspiration from great works of literature. He was also interested in mythology and legend, as seen in his choice of subject matter for *The Merciful Knight* (1863), based on an eleventh-century legend. This painting is from Burne-Jones's first *Pygmalion* series (1867–69). He painted a second version of the series in 1875–78; the first series uses harsher colours and less supple lines. The story of Pygmalion, a Cypriot sculptor, was taken from Ovid's *Metamorphoses*. The Pre-Raphaelite debt to ancient art is seen here by a representation of the Classical statue of the *Three Graces*, bathed in light at the back of Pygmalion's studio.

The Golden Stairs, The Merciful Knight, Sidonia von Bork

Dante Gabriel Rossetti (1828–82)

The Day Dream

Victoria and Albert Museum, London. Courtesy of the Bridgeman Art Library

DANTE GABRIEL ROSSETTI was born in London of Italian parents, and was the elder brother of the poet, Christina (1830–94). Rossetti studied under Ford Madox Brown (1821–93) before sharing a studio with William Holman Hunt (1827–1910). In 1848, the two friends and Sir John Everett Millais (1829–96) set up the Pre-Raphaelite Brotherhood. All three artists became famous in their own right. Millais eventually turned to society portraits and works of crowd-pleasing sentimentality, while Hunt maintained his adherence to religious and spiritual subjects. However, Rossetti's work became more sensual, much of it portraying voluptuous women whose physical presence fills the entire canvas. With little need for background detail, the only ornamentation is in Rossetti's rich palette and the opulent materials and jewels draping his models. Most of Rossetti's models were also his lovers, including Elizabeth Siddal (1829–62), whom Rossetti married after a 10-year relationship, just 18 months before her tragic death. The model for *The Day Dream* and, indeed, for many of his later paintings, was Jane Morris, the wife of William Morris (1834–96). Rossetti had been in love with Jane for many years, and his deluded belief that she was unable to break free from her marriage to be with him is symbolised by the branches that entrap her within the painting.

 Fazio's Mistress, Beata Beatrix, Found

1883 Sir Lawrence Alma-Tadema (1836–1912)

A Declaration: An Old, Old Story
British Museum, London. Courtesy of the Bridgeman Art Library

SIR LAWRENCE ALMA-TADEMA came to England from the Netherlands in 1870. His style of High Victorian Art became extremely popular in late-Victorian Britain, prompting the artist to make a permanent home in England. Although not actually a Pre-Raphaelite painter, Alma-Tadema was influenced by their style and, like them, looked to history and literature for his inspiration.

Often allied with Frederic, Lord Leighton (1830–96), Alma-Tadema was an equally scholarly painter who paid great attention to detail. His background was in Classical academia and, although he was often accused of confusingly combining different periods in history in his paintings, he did so to create stunning artistic effects, rather than because of historical ignorance.

The historical periods most often depicted by Alma-Tadema were those of ancient civilisations, in particular Ancient Greece, Rome, Pompeii and Egypt. His painterly style was opulent and voluptuous; richly coloured and seductive in appearance. His works usually contain portraits of intensely beautiful women in ornate surroundings, painted in either watercolours (as here) or oils. Often, as in *A Declaration: An Old, Old Story*, he places the figures in a marble surround to emphasise the flesh tones and to allow him to experiment with light.

The Meeting of Anthony and Cleopatra 41 BC, Bacchanal, Unconscious Rivals

PRE-RAPHAELITE

William Morris (1834–96)

Iris textile design
Victoria and Albert Museum, London. Courtesy of the Bridgeman Art Library

WILLIAM MORRIS was a painter, designer, businessman, novelist, poet and political activist. While at Oxford University he met Edward Burne-Jones (1833–98), with whom he struck up a life-long friendship and artistic partnership. Morris was born into a wealthy family; he used his legacy to set up the company, Morris and Co., for which Burne-Jones and Rossetti (1828–82), among others, provided designs. The firm produced textiles, tiles, furniture and stained glass. As well as running a successful business, Morris published volumes of poetry and a Utopian novel, *News from Nowhere*. He was also a fervent Socialist.

Despite Morris's attempts to create a Utopian world, his efforts were thwarted by the problems he experienced in his marriage to Jane Burden, one of the Pre-Raphaelites' models. Jane and Rossetti, Morris's greatest mentor and friend, began a sustained affair after the death of Rossetti's wife, Lizzie Siddall, in 1862. Morris was selflessly indulgent, despite the love he felt for Jane, turning a blind eye to the time she and her lover spent in his and Rossetti's joint summer home. *Iris* was one of the textile designs that Morris himself produced for the company. Many of his designs feature flowers or birds, an indication not only of his love for nature but also of the influence of aestheticism on his work.

 Queen Guinevere or *La Belle Iseult*, *Minstrel with Cymbals* (stained glass), *Tulip* pattern (textile)

John William Waterhouse (1849–1917)

Ophelia
Christie's Images, London. Courtesy of the Bridgeman Art Library

JOHN WILLIAM WATERHOUSE was born in Italy, to English parents. He began his career as a painter in the Pre-Raphaelite mould, but went on to create his own style, perhaps best defined as Romantic Classicism. Waterhouse's conscious decision to ally himself with the Pre-Raphaelites can be seen in his duplication of their subjects, such as *Ophelia* and *The Lady of Shalott* (1888), and in his adherence to the teachings contained in Ruskin's *Modern Painters* (1843) – a book from which the Pre-Raphaelites drew inspiration. However, Waterhouse also looked to ancient cultures for material and was influenced by the art of Alma-Tadema (1836–1912) and Lord Leighton (1830–96). Towards the end of his life, his style was to some degree influenced by Impressionism.

Although Waterhouse's career underwent several stylistic changes, his fidelity to accurate portraiture and his interest in the re-creation of natural light remained constant. His paintings are exquisitely detailed and executed with faithful attention to the subject's source, whether historical, mythological or literary.

In this painting, Waterhouse depicts the final moments of Ophelia's life, in contrast to Millais' famous *Ophelia* (1852) in which she has already drowned. Waterhouse balances Ophelia's virginal paleness by the use of funereal background colours.

The Lady of Shalott, St Eulalia, Miranda: The Tempest

Gustave Courbet (1819–77)

Bonjour Monsieur Courbet

Fabre Museum, Montpellier. Courtesy of the Bridgeman Art Library

COURBET was born at Ornans, France. His art was largely self-taught, achieved by studying sixteenth- and seventeenth-century art – in particular the work of Caravaggio (1571–1610) and Rembrandt (1606–69). Courbet was at the forefront of artistic and political activism in nineteenth-century France. In 1873, following a spell in prison as a result of his political activities and inability to pay his debts, Courbet fled to Switzerland. He remained in exile until his death four years later.

In 1855, dissatisfied with the Parisian Salon, Courbet staged an independent exhibition of his works. His political beliefs are evident in the self-portrait included in *Bonjour Monsieur Courbet*, notably in the defiant tilt of his chin and the firm grip on his stick. In this painting Courbet depicts himself (the figure striding on the right) as he is met by his patron, Alfred Bruyas.

The painting (also called *Le Rencontre*) demonstrates why Courbet was hailed as the premier Realist of his day: every detail, such as the braiding on Bruyas' jacket and the buttons on Courbet's walking boots, is minutely finished. Of the three figures, Courbet's self-portait commands most attention as he moves towards the centre of the canvas. The eyes of Bruyas and his dog, as well as those of the viewer, are all drawn towards Courbet.

 Burial at Ornans, The Stone Breakers, The Artist's Studio

Jean-François Millet (1814–75)

The Gleaners

Orsay Museum, Paris. Courtesy of the Bridgeman Art Library

JEAN FRANÇOIS MILLET was born in Normandy, France, the son of a farm labourer. He studied locally with Bon du Mouchel (1807–46), from whom he learned his portrait skills. In 1837 he won a scholarship and moved to Paris to study under the historical painter Paul Delaroche (1797–1856), who passed on his skills to the young Millet.

In 1840 Millet set up his own studio, making a living as a portrait painter. In 1848 he had an overwhelming success with *The Winnower*, which he had exhibited at the Paris Salon. At about the same time he became involved with the Barbizon School, a group of landscape artists led by Théodore Rousseau (1812–67). He moved to Barbizon in 1849 but was never a member of the school, preferring to make people the focus of his landscapes, as in *The Gleaners*. Millet painted many pictures depicting the grim reality of French peasants toiling on the land, seen also in *The Sower* (c. 1850) and *The Angelus* (1857–59), among others. The golden light of Millet's *The Gleaners* throws the peasant women in the foreground of the painting into sharp relief, heightening the sense of pathos. Millet used his paintings to reveal the harshness of poverty and social injustice; as a result he was considered to be a champion of left-wing political groups.

 Bird Hunters, The Sower, The Angelus

Honoré Daumier (1808–79)

The Laundress
Orsay Museum, Paris. Courtesy of the Bridgeman Art Library

HONORÉ DAUMIER was best known in his lifetime as a social satirist. His cartoons, published in left-wing magazines, made his name and he became famous for his satire. He was determined to succeed as an artist outside the limitations of satirical drawing and attempted to gain recognition as a painter and scupltor.

Daumier's works were lauded only after his death. With the new-found interest in Expressionism at the end of the nineteenth century, and with the advent of Impressionism, Daumier's style found appreciative critics, who cited his works as having been an inspiration to both artistic movements.

Towards the end of his life Daumier's sight deteriorated, and he became poverty-stricken. His slide into destitution was curbed

only by the intervention of Corot (1796–1875), who generously provided Daumier with a home.

In an age when Realism required minute attention to detail and 'finish', it is easy to see why *The Laundress*, and other work in a similar style by Daumier, with its blurred outlines and indistinct facial features, was not well received in his lifetime. His subject matter, showing an every-day scene from the life of a lower-class woman, is remininscent of works by Edgar Degas (1834–1917) such as *Women Ironing* (1884).

 Don Quixote, The Painter Before His Easal, The Print Collectors

The Woman of the Pearl

Louvre, Paris. Courtesy of the Bridgeman Art Library

FRENCH-BORN Corot spent much of his life in Paris, although, like most artists of his era, he made visits to Italy between 1825 and 1835 to further his education by studying the Old Masters. Unusually, Corot did not choose painting as a career until he reached his mid-twenties. This was a decision influenced by fellow Frenchman Achille Etna Michallon (1796–1822), who guided Corot's early career and was himself a renowned landscape artist.

Corot is best known for his landscapes, which were in great demand from the wealthy patrons who supported him. His early paintings were strongly influenced by the classical tradition of Arcadian landscapes, but his works such as *Ville d'Avray* (c. 1870) were inspired by the French counryside, marking a move away

from the Italian landscapes of his youth towards a more realistic style. The brushwork in Corot's later paintings often betrays an Impressionistic quality.

Corot produced relatively few portrait studies which, although of a consistently high standard, have been a neglected part of his *oeuvre*. The same applies to his nude figure studies. The dots of pink and yellow flesh tones, used to create light, shadow and form in the face of the model for *The Woman of the Pearl*, also anticipate the Impressionist movement.

 Woman in Blue, View of the Colosseum, Agostina

James Abbot MacNeill Whistler (1834–1903)

Portrait of the Artist's Mother

Orsay Museum, Paris. Courtesy of the Bridgeman Art Library

IN 1859, after studying in Paris, American-born Whistler moved to London. He became renowned for his personality – charming and hostile by turns – as much as for his art. His work often contained elements from the Japanese art which he brought to prominence in Britain, but he was also influenced by nineteenth-century French and British art. He was also a writer and lecturer, publishing a collection of his essays in *The Gentle Art of Making Enemies* (1890).

Whistler was closely involved in London's artistic and literary circles, associating with Rossetti (1828–82) and Oscar Wilde (1854–1901). In 1878 he sued John Ruskin (1819–1900) for libel after he likened Whistler's work to 'a paint pot flung at a canvas'.

Despite winning the case, Whistler was forced into bankruptcy when costs were awarded against him. He left Britain for some years, but eventually returned to settle in London.

Portrait of the Artist's Mother is typical of Whistler's accurate facial portraiture and his use of blocks of colour. His subjects were seldom named; instead the works bore titles indicated by the colours worn by the sitter, such as *Symphony in White No. 2* (1864). The alternative title for this picture is *Arrangement in Grey and Black No. I*.

 Nocturne in Black and Gold: the Falling Rocket, Chelsea Shops, Harmony in Green

Winslow Homer (1836–1910)

Breezing Up

National Gallery of Art, Washington DC. Courtesy of the Bridgeman Art Library

WINSLOW HOMER was one of the foremost American Realist artists. He was also an illustrator and journalist. He worked in oils and watercolours and produced etchings. His early paintings are predominantly in oils but, from the early 1880s, he began producing watercolours almost exclusively.

Homer lived for a time in New York, but he was always happier by the sea. He travelled to England in 1881, where he spent time painting watercolours of English coastal scenes. In 1881–82, back in America, he bought a house near the Atlantic coast at Prout's Neck, where he lived in isolation. His early paintings had been mainly of rural scenes, but in the mid-1880s he switched to sea pictures, such as *Fog Warning* (1885) and *The Life Line* (1884),

both of which portray the sea as an angry life-threatening force. He also had a great talent for producing unsentimental pictures of animals, such as *Fox Hunt* (1893) and *Deer Drinking* (1892).

In *Breezing Up*, the sea is choppy but unthreatening, calling to mind long, lazy school holidays and childhood adventure. The little yacht was named 'Gloucester', after a town on the Maine coast which was a favourite holiday spot for Homer and other artists in the 1870s.

 Prisoners from the Front, Cotton Pickers, Gloucester Farm

REALIST

John Singer Sargent (1856–1925)

Luxembourg Gardens at Twilight
Minneapolis Institute of Art, Minnesota. Courtesy of the Bridgeman Art Library

SARGENT was an American citizen, although he was born in Italy. He spent much of his youth travelling, before settling in London in 1884. His influences were diverse, ranging from the works of Velàzquez (1599–1660) and Frans Hals (c. 1582–1666) to his Impressionist contemporaries. His awareness of the most up-to-date movements in French art is unsurprising, since his artistic education was in France, under Carolus-Duran (1838–1917).

In London, Sargent earned fame as a portraitist, receiving more commissions than he could possibly accept. Those he undertook, such as *Eva and Betty Wertheimer* (1901) and *The Misses Vickers* (1886), reveal his genius for re-creating facial idiosyncracies, as well as his understanding of the human form. In the later years of

his life, however, he was able to return to his first love – landscape painting – when he took extended holidays from London to paint the British countryside. During the First World War he was appointed as the official War Artist. The horrors of war are evoked in Sargent's disturbing *Gassed* (1918).

Luxembourg Gardens at Twilight demonstrates the affinity Sargent felt for the Impressionist movement. With its pointillistic light effects, it is in marked contrast to his sharply detailed portraits and the exquisite clarity of *Carnation, Lily, Lily, Rose* (1885–86).

 Gassed, Portrait of Madame X, Carnation, Lily, Lily, Rose

Ignace Henri Jean
Fantin-Latour (1836–1904)

White and Pink Roses
Christie's Images, London. Courtesy of the Bridgeman Art Library

FANTIN-LATOUR was born in Grenoble, France, of an Italian father and Russian mother. His father, also an artist, tutored the young Fantin-Latour for the first years of his life. At the age of 14, he was enrolled in art school and later became a pupil of Courbet (1819–77). Elements of Courbet's technique, along with that of Corot (1796–1875), Delacroix (1798–1863), Titian (c. 1487–1576) and Veronese (c. 1528–88), can be found in Fantin-Latour's work, although his subject matter differed from theirs. He is best known for his flower studies, although he painted occasional portrait groups as well as historical scenes and landscapes.

Fantin-Latour travelled a little in Europe, but always returned to France. He was promenent in the intellectual and artistic society of late nineteenth-century France – being on good terms with Whistler (1834–1903), Manet (1832–83) and all the Impressionist artists – yet he retained his individual style, exhibiting mainly detailed still lifes and never taking up the lucrative profession of society portraitist.

White and Pink Roses demonstrates Fantin-Latour's meticulous technique: the gently frilled petals, each formed by a single stroke of paint, are almost photographic in their realism.

 To the Betrothed, Homage to Manet, Homage to Delacroix

Thomas Cowperthwait Eakins (1844–1916)

Between Rounds

Philadelphia Museum of Art, Pennsylvania. Courtesy of the Bridgeman Art Library

EAKINS was born in the US and studied at the Pennsylvania Academy. In the mid-1860s he travelled to Europe, where he was deeply influenced by the art he encountered, in particular that of Velàzquez (1599–1660). In 1870, Eakins returned home and became a director of the Pennsylvania Academy, a post from which he later resigned after a scandal caused by his insistence that female students should draw the male figure from nude models.

Like many artists of his time, he was fascinated by photography; his later works, such as *Between Rounds*, reveal his attempt to inject photographic realism into his paintings. This adherence to Realism and his refusal to pander to popular aesthetic ideals prevented him becoming fashionable during his lifetime, although his considerable artistic ability was recognised.

Between Rounds portrayed a far seamier side of life than the American art-buying public cared to see: the grim determination of the boxer and the threat of a disturbance implicit in the presence of the policeman were not considered suitable subjects for painting at that time. Eakins' determination to show the more disturbing side of life was underlined by his 1875 painting, *The Gross Clinic*, which shows a harrowingly realistic portrayal of a contemporary operating theatre.

 Masked Woman Seated, The Gross Clinic, Baseball Players Practising

Édouard Manet (1832–83)

Luncheon on the Grass

Orsay Museum, Paris. Courtesy of the Bridgeman Art Library

MANET was born in Paris to wealthy parents and his artistic talents were apparent early in his life. In 1850, after a short stint in the French navy, he joined the studio of Thomas Couture (1815–79), a Neo-Classical painter who steered his students away from an obsessive attention to detail.

Manet's work was remarkable for its modernity, both in terms of technique and subject matter – qualities that attracted the admiration of a younger group of painters who came to be known as the Impressionists. Despite challenging the views of the art establishment, Manet craved official acceptance for his work. Consequently, he never exhibited with the Impressionists, although his work influenced their development. Manet spent much time with members of the Impressionist group in the cafés of Paris, and during the 1870s he painted in an Impressionist style. Much of his subject matter was also in keeping with the spirit of his contemporary, Edgar Degas (1834–1917).

Luncheon on the Grass marked a turning point in French painting. Based on a work by the Italian Old Master Giorgione (c. 1477–1510), it caused a scandal in the art world because of the way it challenged Classical motifs.

In 1883, Manet's achievements were recognised by the state when he was awarded the legion d'Honneur.

🐚 *Music in the Tuileries, Olympia, Bar at the Folies Bergère*

Eugène Boudin (1824–1898)

The Beach at Trouville
Orsay Museum, Paris. Courtesy of the Bridgeman Art Library

BOUDIN was apprenticed to a printer in Le Havre and painted in his spare time. However, after visiting northern France and Flanders in 1848 and exhibiting two of his pictures, he enrolled at the École des Beaux-Arts in Paris, where he studied from 1851–53. He exhibited at the Salon of 1859, where his work was admired by Symbolist poet Charles Baudelaire (1821–67).

Boudin was a follower of French landscape and figure painter Jean-Baptiste-Camille Corot (1796–1875) and spent most of his career painting along the coast of northern France. He was one of the first artists to advocate painting in the open air (rather than sketching outside and producing a finished composition in the studio), an idea he introduced to Claude Monet (1840–1926) in

1858. Boudin's work was an extremely important influence on the early career of Monet.

From 1870, Boudin's brushwork became broader. In his later years, he began to use brighter, richer colours. From 1862 he was a regular visitor to Trouville, where he painted this composition of the French upper classes at leisure by the sea. The painting has many features that are typical of Boudin's work, including the use of small figures, the lack of a central subject, the play of light on the water and the broad, atmospheric sky.

 Beach Scene, Sailing Ships at Deauville, Fishing Huts with Jetty

Berthe Morisot (1841-95)

Portrait of the Artist's Mother and Sister
National Gallery of Art, Washington DC. Courtesy of the Bridgeman Art Library

MORISOT, the daughter of a top civil servant and great-great-niece of the rococo artist Jean-Honoré Fragonard (1732–1806), grew up in a cultured environment. Between 1860 and 1862 she was a pupil of French landscape painter Jean-Baptiste-Camille Corot (1796–1875), who advised her to paint out of doors. She came into contact with the Impressionists through Èdouard Manet (1832–83), whom she befriended in 1869. She married Manet's brother and persuaded Manet to experiment with painting outside, to abandon his predominant use of black and to adopt a lighter, Impressionist palette.

Morisot exhibited at all but one of the Impressionist exhibitions. She excelled at portraits and domestic scenes, which she imbued with a spontaneity and light, airy quality. She always worked in the Impressionist style and had a rare understanding of tonal harmony. She was also highly skilled in the use of watercolours.

She exhibited this early painting at the first independent Impressionist exhibition in 1874. It is a daring design with the stark contrast between her sister in dazzling white, lit from the window, and mother, wearing black, who takes up the foreground and almost half of the picture space. The composition is cut off and the mirror is off-centre, revealing the influence of photography and Japanese prints on Morisot's painting.

Hide-and-Seek, Young Woman Powdering Herself, Young Girl

Frédéric Bazille (1841–70)

The Artist's Studio

Orsay Museum, Paris. Courtesy of the Bridgeman Art Library

BAZILLE came from a middle-class family in the Languedoc region of southern France. In 1859 he began medical studies in Montpellier. Continuing his studies in Paris in 1862, he also took up painting at the studio of the artist Charles Gleyre (1808–74), studying alongside Claude Monet, Pierre-Auguste Renoir (1884–1919) and Alfred Sisley (1839–99). The group often travelled together to locations outside Paris to paint in the open air.

In 1864, Bazille gave up medicine and took up painting full time. He shared studios with both Monet and Renoir and first exhibited at the Salon of 1866. His varied work is characterised by its bright colours and limpid atmosphere. Tragically, he died in the Franco-Prussian War (1870–71) before Impressionism had

been fully developed. His influences included Édouard Manet (1832–83) and Gustave Courbet (1819–77); some of his subject matter, such as the nude study in *After the Bath* (1870), although clearly influenced by the Old Masters, suggests his willingness to take a more modern approach.

Painted the year he died, *The Artist's Studio* shows Bazille experimenting with an unusual group composition, in which he was heavily influenced by the Japanese prints becoming available in Paris at about this time.

 Self-Portrait, Family Reunion, After the Bath

Alfred Sisley (1839–99)

Port Marly – White Frost

Beaux-Arts Museum, Lille. Courtesy of the Bridgeman Art Library

ALFRED SISLEY was English but was born in Paris, to wealthy parents. He had planned to be a businessman but in 1857 began to draw. In 1862 he met Monet, Bazille and Renoir at Charles Gleyre's studio in Paris. With them, he painted in the open air in the woods near the village of Barbizon.

An enthusiastic follower of Monet, Sisley was a committed landscape artist. Of all the Impressionists, he experimented the least with his style and technique, painting in the same manner throughout his career, although there is a more brittle quality to his later work. Sisley's main focus was to paint the landscape around him, usually seen from a distance and disappearing to a vanishing point on the horizon.

Sisley died of cancer in 1899, and his finances were in such a poor state that his fellow artists made a collection for his children. At a posthumous auction of his works, however, the prices – so low in his lifetime – rose dramatically.

The informal brushwork in this painting varies in style and technique, according to Sisley's belief that a painting should exhibit a variety of treatment, corresponding to the needs of the subject matter and the effect being sought. This is one reason why Impressionist paintings create such a feeling of vitality.

St Martin Canal, Snow at Suresnes, Moret-sur-Loing in Morning Sun

Edgar Degas (1834–1917)

The Ballet Rehearsal

MOMA, New York. Courtesy of the Bridgeman Art Library

EDGAR Degas came from a wealthy family and trained initially as a historical painter. However, his interest in modern motifs became apparent in the early1860s, when he began to paint racecourses. He was also a gifted portrait painter, showing a rare insight into the character of his sitters. From early on, Degas' work is almost abstract in its concern for design and pattern and its use of unusual viewpoints. In 1869, he exhibited at the official Paris Salon for the last time, exhibiting independently thereafter.

Degas was instrumental in organising the first independent Impressionist exhibition in 1874 and was involved in all but one of their subsequent exhibitions. Many of his contemporary motifs proved offensive to the public. At the Impressionist exhibition of 1886 his pastels of women at their toilette (perfectly acceptable in a classical setting) caused uproar. This painting is an example of Degas' pictures of dancers. He used them to express pattern and movement, often repeating poses drawn from memory or traced from earlier sketches. He often combined several media – this oil painting shows traces of watercolour and pastel. His work was influence by Japanese prints and the new medium of photography.

From the 1890s, as his eyesight began to deteriorate, Degas painted loose images in pastel, and produced models in wax.

 The Belleli Family, The Tub, Blue Dancers

Gustave Caillebotte (1848–94)

Pont de L'Europe
Petit Palais, Geneva. Courtesy of the Bridgeman Art Library

A NAVAL engineer and amateur painter, Caillebotte studied as a portraitist and historical painter. He met Edgar Degas (1834–1917) and Pierre-Auguste Renoir (1841–1919) in 1874. He came from a wealthy family and throughout his career supported the other Impressionists, in particular by helping to finance exhibitions and buying many of the canvases himself. Caillebotte's early work bears affinities with that of Èdouard Manet (1832–83) and Degas, both realist painters of city life. Like Manet, Caillebotte's figures are part of his modern setting and not simply vehicles for the effects of light and colour, as with other Impressionist painters.

His works are notable for their interesting compositions, often viewed from unusual angles and with part of the image 'cut off', as if in a photograph. Until the 1880s, Caillebotte took his images from the world around him – street scenes, family portraits, working-class life and scenes on the River Yerres where he took holidays. His work became more Impressionist in style and in 1882 he retired from public life, painting only landscapes and still lifes.

This painting is interesting for its composition, with movement in and out of the painting. The dog walks away from the viewer while the couple appear to be walking out of the picture.

 The Floor Strippers, Street in the Rain, Snow-Covered Roofs in Paris

Pierre-Auguste Renoir (1841–1919)

The Boating Party

Phillips Collection, Washington DC. Courtesy of the Bridgeman Art Library

RENOIR, who began his career a porcelain painter, was a founder member of Impressionism, with Monet, in 1860. Bazille and Alfred Sisley soon joined the group and from 1863 they began to work out of doors near Barbizon, where Renoir also befriended Camille Pissarro (1830–1903) and Paul Cézanne (1839–1906).

He exhibited at the first three Impressionist exhibitions and at the seventh. Otherwise, he showed his work at private one-man exhibitions and at the Paris Salon. Until the 1890s, Renoir was generally more interested in painting people than landscapes. Unlike some of the other Impressionists, he favoured society portraits and pictures of the middle-classes at play. He painted with soft, caressing, almost sensual, brushstrokes – there is no trace of the darker undertones found in the work of Èdouard Manet (1832–83) and Edgar Degas (1834–1917).

Renoir became dissatisfied with his style and in 1881 travelled to North Africa and Italy. For a few years he practised a harder, more 'classical' style, in which forms were far more clearly delineated and the brushwork less free.

From about 1890 he returned to his softer style, and painted mainly nudes and landscapes. In 1900 he was awarded the legion d'Honneur and his work was increasingly shown abroad.

 La Grenouillère, Madame Charpentier and her Children, Bathers

Mary Cassatt (1844–1926)

Young Woman Sewing in the Garden (1880–82)

Orsay Museum, Paris. Courtesy of the Bridgeman Art Library

MARY CASSATT, a wealthy American artist, studied at the Pennsylvania Academy of Arts between 1861 and 1865. She came to Paris in 1866. Largely self-taught, she first exhibited at the official Salon in 1868. She then returned to the US for a while, and toured Italy during the Franco-Prussian War (1870–71). She exhibited at the Paris Salon again in 1872 and travelled in Europe during 1873, when she came into contact with the work of Velázquez (1599–1660), Rembrandt (1606–69) and Rubens (1577–1640) – all superb colourists whom she greatly admired.

Cassatt was introduced to Edgar Degas (1834–1917) in 1877; both he and Renoir (1841–1919) were important influences on her work. She took part in several of the independent Impressionist exhibitions in Paris and was largely responsible for introducing the Impressionists to several wealthy American collectors.

She painted in oils and from 1890 also produced high-quality prints, making effective use of her understanding of line and drawing. However, she is particularly known for her insightful pictures of women, often with their children. This painting is fairly typical in its content and style, but note how Cassatt implies height in such a way that the background seems like a flat-patterned backdrop – undoubtedly a skill learned from Degas.

Little Girl in a Blue Armchair, Mother about to Wash her Sleepy Child, The Boating Party

Camille Pissarro (1830–1903)

Woman Hanging up the Washing

Palais de Tokyo, Paris. Courtesy of the Bridgeman Art Library

PISSARRO was born in the West Indies, although he had Danish nationality. The oldest of the Impressionists, he went to Paris in 1885, where he painted in the manner of the landscapist Gustave Courbet (1819–77). He was a founder member of the Impressionist group, and the only one to exhibit at all eight independent exhibitions. Pissarro was highly influential in the early work of Paul Cézanne (1839–1906), who worked with him at Louveciennes for ten years. From 1888, he suffered with eye problems and stopped working in the open air. Instead, he concentrated on views of city life, usually painted looking down from hotel windows. In 1889, with the other Impressionists, he exhibited at the Paris World Fair. During the 1890s his work became increasingly well known.

Between the mid-1880s and 1890, under the influence of Georges Seurat (1859–91), Pissarro painted in the 'scientific' divisionist or pointillist style. From the 1880s, he also began to concentrate on figures as the subjects of his work. *Woman Hanging up the Washing* shows Pissarro's new style and the dabs of colour used in pointillism. However, although Pissarro achieves a monumentality of sorts, he does not adhere to the pointillist system completely and his work still retains the freshness and spontaneity typical of Impressionism.

The Hermitage at Pontoise, Woman in an Orchard, Spring Sunshine in a Field, Eragny

William Merritt Chase (1849–1916)

A Friendly Visit

National Gallery of Art, Washington DC. Courtesy of the Bridgeman Art Library

WILLIAM Merritt Chase was one of the earliest proponents of the Impressionist style in the US and the foremost teacher of his generation, teaching American artists such as Georgia O'Keeffe (1887–1986), Charles R. Sheeler (1883–1965), and Charles Demuth (1883–1935). His wide-ranging subject matter – still lifes, portraits, interiors and landscapes – reflected everyday life.

He studied in the US but went to Munich in 1872 after winning a scholarship. He returned in 1878, with an already established reputation, to teach at the Art Students' League of New York. However, he resigned as a result of clashes with the conservative board of governors, setting up his own Chase School of Art in 1896 (which later became the famous New York School of Art).

In 1881 he visited Paris and discovered Impressionism. Chase moved away from the tonal style he had learned in Munich, using a much brighter palette and painting outside. During the 1890s he painted in an increasingly Impressionist style, keeping abreast of developments in Impressionism through exhibitions organised in New York by French art dealer Paul Durand-Ruel (1831–1922).

Here Chase highlights the social niceties of an afternoon conversation between two elegant women, simply but expensively dressed in white, against a darker background.

 Idle Hours, Portrait of Whistler, English Cod

Walter Richard Sickert (1860–1942)

Nude Before a Mirror, Mornington Crescent

Private Collection. Courtesy of the Bridgeman Art Library

SICKERT was a painter, printmaker and engraver, the son of a Danish-German father and an Anglo-Irish mother. He was the most important British Impressionist, although like Edgar Degas (1834–1917) and Rex Whistler (1905–44), with whom he became friends, his work was not typical of the Impressionist style.

Sickert initially trained as an actor but began to paint in 1881, when he became a pupil of Whistler. From Whistler he learned the use of subtle tones, although his palette was generally richer than that of his master. Whistler also taught him to etch. In 1883 Sickert went to Paris where he met Degas, who impressed upon him the importance of both draughtsmanship and freedom of composition. In 1888 Sickert joined the New English Art Club in London,

which had been set up in response to the Royal Academy's conservative attitudes. He became the link between the French and British avant-garde and set up the Camden Town Group (1911–13), which produced paintings of urban scenes with a broadly impressionistic handling. From 1905, Sickert painted nudes, and urban and figure compositions, especially of the theatre, music halls and sombre domestic interiors. This nude study, with the canvas showing through in places (another Impressionist technique), shows the broad brushstrokes that were typical of Sickert's work.

 Lion Comique, The City Atlas, Boredom

Claude Monet (1840–1926)

Waterlilies
Private Collection. Courtesy of the Bridgeman Art Library

CLAUDE MONET was born in Le Havre. In 1859 he moved to Paris, where he met Bazille, Pissarro, Sisley and Renoir. They soon began painting together outdoors. Unlike Manet and Degas, Monet was not concerned with painting the realities of modern life. His interest lay in nature and the fleeting, natural effects of light. Monet's few paintings of interiors and his images of city life are merely an excuse to study light in a different environment.

Success was long in coming and for many years his family suffered hardship. His first wife, Camille, died of cancer in 1879 and thereafter he lived with Alice Hoschedé, the wife of a bankrupt former patron.

Monet is best known for his series paintings, in which he explored particular subjects in differing light conditions at various times of day, most famously his series of haystacks, poplar trees and Rouen Cathedral. His waterlily paintings, produced almost exclusively from 1899 when he moved to Giverny, just outside Paris, are a natural progression of this. As his eyesight deteriorated, his work became increasingly abstract, as here, with everything except the lilies and the reflective surface of the water was eliminated.

Monet died an artistic rebel, an inspiration for the abstract movement and the new avant-garde.

🖼 *Women in the Garden, Lady with Parasol, Rouen Cathedral in the Morning Sun (Harmony in Blue)*

Pierre-Cecile Puvis de Chavannes (1824–98)

Poor Fisherman

Courtesy of the Bridgeman Art Library

FRENCH-BORN Puvis de Chavannes studied in Italy with Delacroix. As a result, his monumentally scaled work had more in common with Italian Renaissance frescoes than with contemporary French Impressionist painting. His huge, mural-like canvases were admired by Symbolist poets Charles Baudelaire and Stéphane Mallarmé (1842–98), and his boldly flat, decorative style was adopted by Gauguin and painters of the Nabi school.

The Symbolists used painting to express social comment, often combined with religious overtones, which endowed art with a sense of inner necessity, or objective meaning – a concept that led to the development of Abstract art. In *Poor Fisherman*, the simple linear effect and pale, almost monotone, palette anticipate Pablo

Picasso's (1881–1973) 'blue' period, which was undoubtedly influenced by Puvis de Chavannes' work. When the picture was first exhibited it was attacked for its unnatural, anaemic colours. The weak light falls down the centre of the painting, while the rest of the scene is plunged into gloom, with the exception of the light-flooded figure of the baby. Puvis de Chavannes quickly won the admiration of Impressionists and Aesthetes, who admired his apparent disregard for the prevailing artistic trend towards realism and his development of Symbolist notions of dreams and visions.

 The Inspiring Muses, Death and the Maidens, Summer

Gustave Moreau (1826–98)

Galatea

Private Collection. Courtesy of the Bridgeman Art Library

A CLASSICALLY trained academic artist, Moreau was a major force in the creation of the Symbolist movement. His intense, magical oil paintings and watercolours were often inspired by visions. As a teacher at the authoritative École des Beaux-Arts in Paris, his views on colour had a profound impact on his pupil, Henri Matisse (1869–1954), as well as on the Fauves and Surrealists.

The Symbolist movement was allied to Aestheticism, which developed early Romantic ideals combined with a taste for the morbid, represented in Britain by Aubrey Beardsley (1872–1898) and Oscar Wilde (1845–1900). Moreau was criticised for his pseudo-romantic tricks, exemplified by his interest in the *femme fatale*, as explored in his *Salome Dancing Before Herod* (1876).

In *Galatea*, Moreau explores the symbolic potential of another favourite mythological siren. According to legend, Galatea fell in love with a humble shepherd, Acis, but was pursued by a three-eyed cyclops who had fallen in love with her. In order to escape from the three-eyed monster, she turned Acis into a river and dived into the water. In this brooding piece, the 'dream state' is not a representation of the subconscious, as in twentieth-century Surrealism; rather, it is triggered by sensual experience and represents an escape from the mundane.

Salome Dancing Before Herod, Hercules and the Hydra of Lerna, The Unicorns

SYMBOLIST

Odilon Redon (1840–1916)

The Cyclops

Rijksmuseum Kröller-Müller, Otterlo. Courtesy of the Bridgeman Art Library

FRENCH artist and writer Odilon Redon began his artistic life as a Realist landscape painter, influenced by Courbet and Corot. By the 1880s and 90s he was hailed as the quintessential Symbolist artist. He knew the Symbolist poets Baudelaire and Mallarmé, and, in common with the movement's other artists, his work reflected Symbolist literature. The Symbolists' 1886 manifesto refuted the Impressionist's visual emphasis on nature – preferring contemplation of the realities of the imagination by the use of symbolism, patterns and images. The spiritual dimension of their work often had political meaning, and sometimes verged on anarchism. Redon was fascinated with expressions of mysticism and influenced the Nabis painters with the flat-patterned charcoal drawings and lithography of his later years. The Nabis school had an effect on the Abstract movement through Surrealist painters such as Francis Picabia (1878–1953). The severed head was a recurring motif in Redon's work, as were the metamorphic myths, such as Galatea. Beheading and transformation each represented spiritual separation and artistic transcendence to a creative, eternal world. In contrast with the monster in Moreau's Galatea, Redon's cyclops is not a dominant figure but a pathetic, phallic-headed monster who cannot resist the sophistication of Galatea.

 Ophelia Among the Flowers, The Red Sphinx, Sita

Gustav Klimt (1862–1918)

The Kiss
Osterreichische Gallery, Vienna. Courtesy of the Bridgeman Art Library

KLIMT was the founding father and a leading member of the Vienna Secession movement, a group of artists who consciously rejected the academic style of the late nineteenth century. He was celebrated for rich, complex, gold-dazzling friezes and portraits of powerful, chic women from Vienna's turn-of-the-century society. Klimt's artistic vocabulary drew on a wealth of Symbolist imagery, incorporating esoteric design and eroticism. Because of this, his work did not always find favour with in the Viennese art world.

Instead, Klimt found extensive patronage abroad, completing the famous Belgian Stoclet Frieze in 1911. This Art Nouveau masterpiece, made for the Wiener Werkstätte arts and crafts guild movement, was influenced by William Morris and Charles Rennie Mackintosh (1868–1928). His early work included impressionistic landscape studies, painted during holidays in the Austrian Alps.

Klimt's exquisite language reached its artistic culmination in his seminal work, *The Kiss*, a celebration of his deeply held belief in the transforming power of idealised love. The painting was produced after Klimt's visit to the Byzantine mosaics in Ravenna, Italy, and was one of his few 'Golden Period' pieces to survive the ravages of a Nazi fire at the end of the Second World War. His later work was a powerful influence on the German Expressionism of Egon Schiele (1890–1918) and Oskar Kokoschka (1886–1980).

 Judith II, Danaï, Beech Forest I

SYMBOLIST

Georges Seurat (1859–91)

Bathing at Asnières

The National Gallery, London. Courtesy of the Bridgeman Art Library

SEURAT came from a wealthy background and was a highly intelligent, methodical man. He started to paint in about 1881 and exhibited at the last Impressionist exhibition in 1886.

Like many young painters at the time, Seurat learned from Impressionism and then moved on. He was fascinated by the science of light and colour theory, and sought to create a rational, formal art through the application of rules, using colour and line in a prescribed form to create colour and light effects. The style he developed used the primary colours of the spectrum, placed in tiny dots on to a flat, coloured background so that the colours became mixed in the eye of the viewer. Hence, yellow and blue placed close together on the canvas would appear as green when viewed from a distance. This technique was known as pointillism, or divisionism, and was also practised by Paul Signac (1863–1935) and Pissarro.

Bathing at Asnières is an early work and Seurat's first large-scale composition. It shares its subject matter and palette with the Impressionists but its static, monumental quality is reminiscent of the early Renaissance artist Piero della Francesca (c. 1416–92).

Seurat died suddenly at the age of 31, probably from meningitis; by this time he was the acknowledged leader of the avant-garde.

 Sunday Afternoon on the Island of La Grande Jatte, Young Woman Powdering Herself, The Circus

Vincent van Gogh (1853–90)

Sunflowers

The National Gallery, London. Courtesy of the Bridgeman Art Library

VAN GOGH discovered his artistic vocation in 1880, having worked previously as an art dealer and a lay preacher. Vincent lived and painted in the Netherlands until 1885, producing dark images of peasants that emphasised their hardship. In 1886, he moved to Paris and his palette became brighter and more intense.

In 1888 Van Gogh settled in Arles in the south of France, but the years 1888–90 were tumultuous for him. He quarrelled with Paul Gauguin (1848–1903), with whom he had hoped to set up an artist's cooperative, and cut off his own ear. Subsequently he spent time in an asylum at St Rémy before moving to Auvers in 1880 to be near his brother, Theo, who supported him financially all his life. However, on 29 July 1890 he committed suicide. He left over 800 paintings and drawings; his work had an enormous influence on Expressionism, Fauvism and Abstract Art.

Van Gogh was a psychologically tortured individual and this is reflected in the intensity of his work. He became obsessed with the power of colour as a symbol and evolved his own style of great swirling brushstrokes. This version of *Sunflowers* (one of many) was painted during Van Gogh's stay in Arles before his decline into insanity. The entire canvas is based on broad, thickly painted areas of yellows and browns.

 The Potato Eaters, The Night Café, Cornfield with Ravens

POST-IMPRESSIONIST

Le Moulin Rouge

Private Collection. Courtesy of the Bridgeman Art Library

TOULOUSE-LAUTREC came from an aristocratic family. In his teens he broke both his legs and sadly they ceased to grow while his torso continued to mature. He began to paint in the studio of Léon Bonnat (1833–1922) in 1882 and had his own studio in Montmartre at the age of 21.

His early influence was the Impressionists – particularly Degas, who shared his interest in theatre perfomers and his fascination with prints by Japanese artists Hokusai (1760–1849) and Hiroshige (1797–1858), popular in Paris at the time. Likewise, Lautrec also painted brothels, living in one in 1894, and racecourses.

Van Gogh, whom he met in 1886, was another influence, notably for his use of cross-hatching. Gauguin's use of broad, flat colour and

graphic outlines also influenced the posters and lithographs that Lautrec began to produce from the 1890s, and which brought him instant recognition. *Le Moulin Rouge* was his first poster and the seedy atmosphere of the artificial nightlife of Paris was captured in a manner close to caricature. He designed many similar posters, based on two or three colours and characterised by flat areas of colour and a use of black contour lines.

Lautrec became an alcoholic and died young, either from the effects of alcoholism or the syphilis he contracted in his twenties.

 At the Moulin Rouge, The Two Friends, Marcelle Lender Dancing the Bolero in Chiliperic

Paul Gauguin (1848–1903)

Woman with a Flower
Carlsberg Glyptotek, Copenhagen. Courtesy of the Bridgeman Art Library

PAUL GAUGUIN, the son of a French father and Creole mother, began painting in the early 1870s while working as a stockbroker. In1883 he became a full-time artist. He was a friend of Pissarro and exhibited in the last four Impressionist exhibitions, but his painting did not bring financial success. In 1886 he left his family and moved to Pont Aven in Brittany, where he produced *The Vision after the Sermon* (1888), in which he abandoned the Impressionist style altogether and used flat areas of colour as a means of expression.

Gauguin moved to Tahiti in 1891, where he believed he became one with nature, a feeling reflected in his later work, which is influenced by the art of primitive peoples. He lived in the South Pacific until his death – from a combination of syphilis and heart disease – and only occasionally returned to France.

Woman with a Flower is one of Gauguin's first Tahitian paintings. His model is very modestly dressed, revealing the extent of the European influence on the local people. In contrast, his later paintings, depicting the apparent simplicity of life in the South Seas, were highly romanticised. During the last decade of his life he painted richly coloured and stylised pastoral scenes, nudes and some still lifes, often with symbolic or allegorical overtones.

 The Breton Shepherdess, Self-Portrait with Yellow Christ, Two Women on a Beach

Paul Signac (1836–1935)

The Château des Papes, Avignon
Orsay Museum, Paris. Courtesy of Giradoun/the Bridgeman Art Library

SIGNAC began his career as an Impressionist but met Seurat in 1884, when they both exhibited at the first exhibition of the Societé des Artistes Indépendants. He contributed to all nine exhibitions and became president of the society in 1908.

Signac became a friend of Seurat and a follower of his pointillist technique. Signac took on his mantle after he died suddenly in 1891 and became the recognised leader of the Neo-Impressionists – a term coined by the critic Felix Fénéon to signify the group of artists who had been influenced by the Impressionists but who had then moved on to different styles. Signac's palette became increasingly bright and his style less technical. From the 1890s, his style was more decorative and artificial than scientific. In 1899 he published *From Delacroix to Neo-Impressionism*, which was considered the definitive work on the subject of pointillism, although it was more a defense of the style than an accurate history.

After 1900 he abandoned pointillism and began to use small, square dabs of colour. This technique was used to paint *The Château des Papes, Avignon*, which looks as though it is created from pieces of mosaic. Signac executed his paintings in the studio, working from watercolour studies done on site.

 The River Bank, Petiti Anderly, The Dining Room, Portrait of Monsieur Félix Fénéon in 1890

Paul Cézanne (1839–1906)

Mont Sainte-Victoire
Hermitage, St Petersburg. Courtesy of the Bridgeman Art Library

CÉZANNE grew up in Aix-en-Provence and trained as a lawyer. In 1861 he began to study painting at the Académie Suisse in Paris. Between 1862 and 1865, he met and became good friends with several Impressionist painters.

Until about 1870 his work varied in style and motif. In some works he used thick impasto and a palette knife, while for others he used more traditional brushwork, his palette was always dark. Despite these differences in style and content, although his work reveals an early interest in the relationships between different planes and the balance between form and colour. During this period he painted still lifes, portraits, and semi-historical and erotic subjects, all infused with an internal violence.

Under the influence of his mentor Pissarro, Cézanne painted in the Impressionist style between 1870–79. From 1880, however, he developed a new style. He applied paint in repeated parallel brushstrokes to produce a subtle, almost woven, effect. He painted many empty landscapes, including a series of paintings showing Mont Sainte-Victoire, near his home in Aix. He also painted portraits and still lifes, in which he experimented with perspective. Although he never lost sight of his subject matter, Cézanne's work looked forward to the abstraction of the twentieth century and had a huge influence on future generations of artists.

 The Card Players, Apples and Oranges, The Large Bathers

POST-IMPRESSIONIST

Auguste Rodin (1840–1917)

The Kiss (bronze)
Phillips, The International Fine Art Auctioneers, Britain. Courtesy of the Bridgeman Art Library

AUGUSTE RODIN was the most celebrated French sculptor of the nineteenth-century. His works were extraordinary for their realism and expressive quality. His sensitivity in modelling and ability to render movement through the play of light on a sculpted surface were unsurpassed.

Rodin became assistant sculptor at the Sèvres Porcelain Factory in 1864. In 1875, he studied Michelangelo's work in Italy and began to apply elements of his technique – in particular, leaving some areas smooth and others unworked – to his own work. This was the turning point of his career. *The Age of Bronze* (1876) caused controversy at the Salon of 1877 because the figure was deemed so lifelike that he was accused of having taken a cast from a live model.

Rodin also introduced the concept of producing a fragment of the body, such as a head, as a finished piece. His sculptures were the cause of dissent and several of his commissions were rejected.

Rodin's largest work was *The Gates of Hell* (1880–1917), a bronze door based on Ghiberti's *Gates of Paradise*. He designed *The Kiss* (shown here in bronze) and *The Thinker* for the doors and later used them as models for independent sculptures. Both pieces also exists in marble – he employed marble-cutters and casters to begin replicas that he completed himself.

 Danaï, The Burghers of Calais, Victor Hugo

Amedeo Modigliani (1884–1920)

Female Nude

Courtauld Gallery, London. Courtesy of the Bridgeman Art Library

AN Italian painter, sculptor and draughtsman, Modigliani worked mainly in Paris. He studied the Italian Renaissance and is often seen as an heir to Botticelli because of the linear grace of his long, slender figures.

From 1906 he became a familiar figure around the nightspots of Montmartre. He was influenced by African sculpture and Cubism, and by the work of Paul Cézanne (1839–1906) and Pablo Picasso (1881–1973). In 1909 he met the sculptor Constantin Brancusi (1876–1957) and for the next five years spent the majority of his time carving. But with the start of the First World War in 1914, materials were hard to come by so he resumed painting. His subject matter was almost exclusively portraits of his friends and

erotic female nudes. His models were often poor, and he depicted them with tenderness. He used broad blocks of colour, but colour was never the guiding spirit of his art, which was dependent on the purity and expressive quality of his draughtsmanship.

Modigliani lived a penurous life, despite his great talent, and died from tuberculosis in 1920 – a disease not helped by his dissolute lifestyle. 'I am going to drink myself dead,' he said, and promptly did. His mistress Jeanne Hébuterne, who was pregnant with his second child, committed suicide on the day of his funeral.

 Head, Reclining Nude, Gypsy Woman with Baby

Edvard Munch (1863–1944)

The Scream

Nasjonalgalleriet, Oslo © Munch Museum/Munch Estate/BONO, Oslo/DACS 2000. Courtesy of the Bridgeman Art Library

THE work of Norwegian artist Munch is often regarded as a bridge between the Post-Impressionists, such as Van Gogh and Gauguin and the early twentieth-century German Expressionist movement. Indeed, his work was an important influence on the development of the Expressionist movement. Munch studied art at Oslo in 1880–82, and during subsequent visits to Paris and Berlin came into contact with the artistic innovations that helped shape his own theories and style of painting.

Munch's paintings, although ostensibly portraying reality, use distortion and exaggerated colour to express an interior rather than exterior world. His work displays his own turbulent emotions that were eventually to lead to a nervous breakdown in 1908.

Munch adopted the swirling, intensely coloured style of Van Gogh to give his work psychological force and passion. The eddying brush strokes create visual echoes all around his figures, and can be seen in *The Madonna* (1894–95). They help to imbue works such as *The Scream* with a feeling of angst, expressing a destructive energy that is barely contained. *The Scream* is part of three groups of work on the themes of love, suffering and death, which Munch called collectively the *Frieze of Life*.

 The Madonna, The Sick Child, Girls on the Jetty

Paula Modersohn-Becker (1876–1907)

Self-Portrait
Haags Gemeentemuseum, Netherlands. Courtesy of the Bridgeman Art Library

BORN in Dresden, Modersohn-Becker studied art but, at her family's insistence, also trained as a teacher. While studying in Berlin in 1896–98 she met members of an artistic colony who lived in a simple, farming village called Worswede, near Bremen. Modersohn-Becker met her future husband, Otto, at the colony when she moved there in 1898. She died at Worswede from an embolism, three weeks after the birth of her daughter.

Modersohn-Becker left Worswede three times to stay in Paris, where she came into contact with the work of Cézanne, Gauguin and Van Gogh, all of whom proved to be highly influential to her painting. In Gauguin, she found examples of the primitivism for which she strived in her own work. Her use of discrete blocks of

colour is an acknowledgement of her debt to Cézanne, while her animated brushwork is a reminder of the work of Van Gogh.

Using these influences, Modersohn-Becker created a style that combines simply depicted forms with a suggestive use of colour, applied in concentrated brush strokes. Her main themes were single figure studies or self-portraits, such as this one, completed the year she died. Self-portraits were especially popular among Expressionist artists, as they offered an excellent vehicle for exploring ideas of the self.

 Old Poorhouse Woman with a Glass Bottle, Self-Portrait with Amber Necklace, Naked Woman Breast-Feeding Her Child

EXPRESSIONIST

Egon Schiele (1890–1918)

Self-Portrait Nude
Albertina Graphic Collection, Vienna. Courtesy of the Bridgeman Art Library

SCHIELE was born in Lower Austria. He began studying at the Vienna Academy of Fine Arts in 1906, where he was introduced to the members of the artistic avant-garde. In 1907 he met Gustave Klimt, whose impact on his work was obvious.

Schiele soon began to develop his own painfully personal style and came to be regarded as one of the leading Expressionist artists (although he did not identify himself as such), because of the deeply emotional content of his work, often expressed by distorted figures. Schiele died at the age of 28 in the influenza pandemic which spread across Europe just as he was beginning to receive recognition for his work. Schiele was fascinated by Freud's writings on the subconscious, which inspired much of the material for his

paintings. His main themes were portraits, self-portraits and nudes, all giving him scope to analyse inner emotions. There was often an overt eroticism and sexuality in his subjects; several of his paintings are sexually explicit and Schiele served a short jail term for obscenity in 1912.

This self-portrait shows Schiele in a typically contorted, angular pose, emaciated and damaged. He looks down and cowers as if trying to hide in shame at his own nudity.

 Seated Woman with Bent Knee, Albert Paris von Gütersloh, The Family

Franz Marc (1880–1916)

Little Yellow Horses

Staatsgalerie, Stuttgart. Courtesy of the Bridgeman Art Library

GERMAN artist Franz Marc originally studied theology but turned to art in 1900, studying at Munich University. During his time in Munich, Marc became involved with the German Art Noveau movement, known as *Jugendstil*. In 1903 and 1907 he visited Paris, where he was particularly affected by the works of Van Gogh. In 1911, Marc teamed up with Wassily Kandinsky (1866–1944) to found the *Blaue Reiter* (Blue Rider) group, staging exhibitions in 1912 and 1913. *Blaue Reiter* also published an *Almanac* containing some of Marc's art theories.

Marc is generally regarded as an exponent of the German Expressionist movement because of his powerful synthesis of colour and form, but by the end of his career his work was closer in style to the Abstract movement. His career was cut short in 1914 when he began military service; he was killed at Verdun in 1916.

Marc believed in the spirituality of animals and often used animal subjects as vehicles for his artistic exploration. The combination of the rounded, simplistic forms of the horses and the warmth of the yellows and reds in *Little Yellow Horses* manifests Marc's search for an artistic resolution of form and colour, and the depth of his achievement.

 Two Cats, Tiger, House in Landscape

EXPRESSIONIST

Ernst Ludwig Kirchner (1880–1938)

Berlin Street Scene

Brucke Museum, Berlin © by Dr Wolfgang & Ingeborg Henze-Ketterer, Wichtrach/Bern. Courtesy of the Bridgeman Art Library

KIRCHNER was the co-founder of *Die Brücke* (The Bridge), the first grouping of German Expressionist painters, who were based in Dresden. The group was inspired by Gauguin, Van Gogh, Munch and primitive art. They believed that their art would act as a bridge to the art of the past, and aspired to simplicity in colour and also form.

Kirchner was the most successful member of the group, becoming possibly the most famous German Expressionist artist. Largely due to problems caused by his often difficult personality, *Die Brücke* broke up in 1913. Following a nervous breakdown in 1917, he moved to Switzerland. Several of his works, along with paintings by Van Gogh and Picasso (1881–1973), were exhibited as examples of

'Degenerate Art' in a 1937 Nazi exhibition in Munich. Kirchner was deeply upset by this; in 1938 he committed suicide.

By 1911 *Die Brücke* had moved to Berlin. While there, Kirchner made many paintings of city scenes. In *Berlin Street Scene* the fierce colours are less jarring than in other of Kirchner's works but still produce a shocking contrast. The upward movement of the scene is enhanced by the direction of the deliberately frenzied brush strokes. The heavily outlined angular forms, typical of Kirchner's style, suggest constrained yet violent emotion.

 Artist and his Model, Self-Portrait with Cat, Striding into the Sea

Marc Chagall (1887–1985)

Two Clowns on Horseback
Christie's Images, London. Courtesy of the Bridgeman Art Library

BORN in Vitebsk, Russia, into a devout Jewish family, Chagall first studied in St Petersburg while working as a sign painter. His outlook changed when he moved to Paris in 1910, where he met the Symbolist poet Apollinaire and the Cubists. He was introduced to Robert Delaunay's (1885–1941) Orphists by Delaunay's Russian-born artist wife, Sonia. The Orphists were extending Cubism into a greater colour range of circles, segments and rhythmic patterns, which they called 'simultaneity'. Chagall returned home on the outbreak of the First World War and joined the pro-French 'Knave of Diamonds' group, which rebelled against the Moscow art school's directives. He combined his earlier European influences with a love of his Jewish heritage to develop a very personal, mystical style.

It is hard to categorise Chagall's prolific output, which ranged from Cubist, through Expressionist (as in this playful piece) to Surrealist. His marriage to Bella Rosenfeld resulted in an energetic series of love works, including the distinctive and colourful *Two Clowns on Horseback*, which probably resulted from Chagall's close involvement with the Jewish State Theatre during the 1920s. After the 1918 Revolution he was made Director of Vitebsk Art School, creating an avant-garde centre until he was unseated by Malevich. His *oeuvre* included ballet sets, biblical illustrations and stained-glass windows.

Paris Through the Window, I and the Village, The Poet Reclining

Oskar Kokoschka (1886–1980)

What Are We Fighting For?

Kunsthaus, Zurich. Courtesy of the Bridgeman Art Library

KOKOSCHKA was one of the foremost Expressionist painters. He was born in Austria and studied in Vienna from 1905–8, at a time when the city was at the centre of cultural innovation, with intellectuals such as Sigmund Freud (1856–1939) and Arnold Schoenberg (1847–1951) working there. In 1910 Kokoschka moved to Berlin to work as a graphic artist on the magazine *Der Sturm* (The Storm), which focused on the art of the German Expressionists. During this period he began to paint what are termed as his 'psychological portraits': works that seek to illustrate the feelings and emotions of the sitter.

In the face of Nazi opposition to his work, Kokoschka moved to Prague in 1934, and then to London in 1938. He became a British citizen and was awarded a CBE. In 1953 he settled in Switzerland, running art summer schools there for ten years.

In 1915 Kokoschka was wounded while serving in the Austrian army in the First World War. Like many artists of his generation, the horrors of war had a profound effect on him, expressed in his paintings. *What Are We Fighting For?* reflects his anti-war stance and his belief in an increasingly pessimistic outcome for humanity after the Second World War. The painting shows his chaotic brushwork, crowded iconography and emotive range of colour.

 Bride of the Wind, Auguste Forel, Portrait of a 'Degenerate Artist'

1896 Charles Rennie Mackintosh (1868–1928)

Part Seen, Imagined Part
Glasgow University Art Library. Courtesy of the Bridgeman Art Library

BORN in Glasgow, Mackintosh served as an architect's apprentice before becoming leader of the avant-garde, and powerfully influential, Glasgow Group, whose prominent members included his own wife, Margaret, and her sister Frances. In 1891 he won a scholarship to tour Europe, where he absorbed a wide range of art historical influences and came into contact with the French Symbolist movement, the influence of which can be seen in his early mystical watercolours. The Glasgow Group exhibited designs for buildings, as well as interiors and furniture, all over Europe. Their collaborative work had a profound impact on artists such as Klimt, who, with other members of the Vienna Secessionist group, adapted the ideas of Art Nouveau.

This hypnotic design is from a mural series of repeated figures for the Ladies' room at the Buchanan tea rooms in Glasgow, completed in 1897. Mackintosh received instant acclaim as an apostle of Art Nouveau, and went on to develop the concept of a 'design for life' begun by William Morris's earlier Arts and Crafts movement. He was influenced by Pre-Raphaelite painters Rossetti and Burne-Jones. The latter's floral imagery in the 'Briar Rose' series of maidens is at work here, as Mackintosh experiments with typical Art Nouveau organic themes of entwining spermatozoa-like vegetation, symbolising fertility, love and the renewal of life.

Blue and Pink Tobacco Flowers, The Wassail, Coullioure

Édouard Vuillard (1868–1940)

Two Girls Walking

Private Collection © ADAGP, Paris and DACS, London 1999. Courtesy of the Bridgeman Art Library

FRENCH painter Vuillard studied at the Parisian Académie Julian, where he met Pierre Bonnard (1867–1947) and other Nabi group members. He shared a studio with Bonnard; both were affected by Gauguin's Pont-Aven group, with its concentration on flat blocks of colour rather than the traditional three-dimensional approach. Fellow Nabi painter Maurice Denis's (1870–1943) belief that a picture, 'before being a horse, nude or subject is essentially a flat surface covered with colours in a certain order,' was also very influential on Vuillard's work.

Vuillard favoured the decorative settings of homely interior scenes and urban landscapes, which allowed him to reproduce their subtle atmosphere with the use of strong surface patterns. He was influenced by the prevailing interest in Japanese prints and, although his work has suffered comparisons with Bonnard's daring lyricism, he created vibrant, poetic and often sensual paintings.

The intense, vibrant colours of *Two Girls Walking* capture a moment of girlhood togetherness within a decorative patchwork of structural forms. The modest scene and apparent simplicity of style obscures the technical mastery of the piece. Sadly, Vuillard's best work had been completed by the turn of the twentieth century. In his last years he withdrew from life, seldom exhibiting after 1914.

 Woman Reading in the Evening, Mother and Child, Artist's Mother and Sister in the Studio

NABI

Pierre Bonnard (1867–1947)

The Open Window
Phillips Collection, Washington DC. Courtesy of the Bridgeman Art Library

FRENCH painter Bonnard studied in Paris, where he met Vuillard and other members of the Nabi group (Nabi is the Hebrew word for 'prophets'). The group developed from Paul Gauguin's Brittany-based Pont-Aven school, which concentrated on flat-patterned composition. The Nabi first exhibited at the Café Volpini in 1889, when Bonnard received acclaim for his early graphic work, in particular his screen printing, in which the influences of Art Nouveau and Japanese prints were apparent. He advocated the Nabi doctrine of abandoning three-dimensional representation in favour of areas of flat colour, although he never truly adopted the movement's Symbolist objectives. Bonnard preferred to explore the creative implications of observation rather than imagination.

His obsessive love for his wife resulted in a series of voyeuristic bath paintings, in which his forms gradually dissolve into pools of transparent light. Matisse's celebrated use of colour blocking had a powerful influence on Bonnard, leading him to explore the decorative effects of colour and eventually resulting in his fluid depiction of light. In *The Open Window* Bonnard deploys bands of colour and a red-green polarisation to create an intensely vibrant sensation of shimmering light, framed by the structural device of the open window. The work is from a series of visions from his later period, which he spent working in the south of France.

Mirror on the Washstand, Nude in the Bathroom, The Table

André Derain (1880–1954)

Charing Cross Bridge
Orsay Museum, Paris. Courtesy of the Bridgeman Art Library

ONE of the original Fauve group, Derain took up painting against his parents' wishes, first working in his Chatou studio with Maurice de Vlaminck (1876–1958) and then with Fauve leader, Henri Matisse (1869–1954), in the south of France. Derain exhibited with the avant-garde group in the famous Salon d'Automne of 1905; the exhibition was brought to the UK by painter-art historian Roger Fry (1866–1934), when the works were labelled for the first time as 'Post-Impressionist'. Derain initially flirted with Neo-Impressionism, expressed in the pointillism of Seurat and Pissaro, who applied pure colour in small dots in a scientifically based chromatic schema. The technique was subsumed by the Fauves (literally, the 'Wild Beasts'), who advanced new conceptual arrangements based on childlike simplicity of form, flat patterns and freedom of line. Under the influence of Van Gogh and Gauguin, pure colour became all-important.

In *Charing Cross Bridge*, the sensational application of colour supersedes any concern for depth of field, as the free flowing lines add a dynamic distribution of movement. Although fascinated with colour, Derain is often seen as the bridge between Matisse and Picasso. He worked alongside Georges Braque (1882–1963) and Picasso studying African and Cézannesque forms, which led to the development of Cubism.

 Banks of the Seine at Pecq, Lady in a Chemise, The Pool of London

Henri Matisse (1869–1954)

The Dance

Hermitage, St Peterburg © Succession H Matisse/DACS 2000. Courtesy of the Bridgeman Art Library

ACKNOWLEDGED as a twentieth-century 'great', critics locate Matisse as the revolutionary master of colour, while Picasso is the revolutionary master of form. The leader of the Fauves, Matisse stormed on to the art scene in the now celebrated 1905 Salon d'Automne exhibition. He initially studied law, becoming a clerk before he turned to art when his tutor, the Symbolist artist Gustave Moreau, allowed him into the École des Beaux-Arts without taking the entrance examination. Such a late start meant that his skills were more rudimentary than those of his contemporaries, but this gave his work a naive charm that he exploited in his later colour experiments. His early works were restrained until he discovered the work of the pointillists, whose free approach towards colour redirected the course of his painting. The celebrated *Luxe, Calm et Volupté* (1904–5) is an experiment in patterned surfaces that underlined his lifelong search for 'balance, purity and serenity'.

During his Post-Impressionist phase, Matisse developed structural strength through the study of primitive art. But when Picasso and the Cubists revolutionised the expression of form, Matisse continued to explore how colour's decorative effects could dictate form, shape and light. In *La Danse*, for example, he uses just three colours to create such an incandescent vibrancy that the dancers appear to leap off the canvas.

 Madame Matisse, Portrait with a Green Stripe, Luxury I

FAUVIST

Maurice de Vlaminck (1876–1958)

The Boats

Christie's Images, London. Courtesy of the Bridgeman Art Library

BORN to Flemish parents, Vlaminck moved to Paris at the age of three. He worked as a writer, busker-violinist and odd-jobber until, at the age of 23 and with no formal training, he took up painting. Unfettered by the established protocol of formalised Classical art, he relished his freedom of style and sense of energy. He often played on this, only acknowledging Van Gogh as an inspiration for his 'savage' approach. He shared a studio with André Derain in Chatou on the river Seine and became a member of the Fauve group through Derain's connection with Matisse. His wild work, exhibited in the 1905 Salon d'Automne, inspired one critic, who was so angered by the 'violent' paintings, to coin the name Les Fauves ('Wild Beasts') to refer to the group.

Vlaminck declared that instinct was the foundation of art. 'I try to paint with my heart and loins,' he said, proud of calling himself a barbarian. He was the first painter to collect African masks, which added a savage intensity to his style.

Strong pointillist influences are evident in *Les Barques*, resulting in long strokes of colour, heightened tones and a bold, violent surface texture. Vlaminck has controlled this intense energy to create real fluidity of movement in the bottom half of the painting, adding a superb shimmering dimension to the river.

 Houses on the Banks of the Seine at Chatou, Landscape with Red Trees, The Bar Counter

Raoul Dufy (1877–1953)

The Paddock at Chantilly
Daniel Malingue Gallery, Paris. Courtesy of the Bridgeman Art Library

DUFY came from a poor family but from a young age was always passionately interested in drawing, enrolling at 5 at the local Le Havre School of Fine Arts. Here he met Cubist pioneer and life-long friend, Georges Braque. (1882–1963). Both men eventually finished their studies in Paris. In 1905 Dufy became fascinated with the colour experiments of Matisse, as seen in the celebrated Salon d'Automne exhibition. He joined the Fauves, helping to develop the group's interest in geometric shapes and the decorative effects of colour. By 1910 he had adopted the formal approach of Cézanne, and his work became more structured. However, this led to a severe monotone palette and the abandonment of bright colours during an unprofitable, sober phase.

Dufy illustrated books for Symbolist poet Guillaume Apollinaire (1880–1918) and teamed up with fashion designer Paul Poiret, creating a textile manufacturing business. In the 1920s, he moved on to colour lithography work. In 1936 he received a commission to produce the world's then largest painting for the Paris World Fair; on the theme of science and electricity, it was 70 metres (200 ft) long. Dufy later reverted to his love of painting, resulting in the highly energetic palette seen in his Fauve-like series on casinos, regattas and racecourses.

Sailing Boats in the Port at Deauville, Placards at Trouville, Old Houses on the Dock at Honfleur

FAUVIST

Francis Picabia (1879–1953)

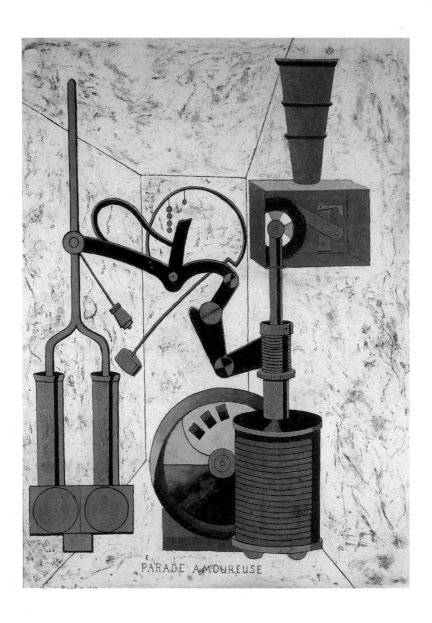

Parade Amoureuse

Private Collection. Courtesy of the Bridgeman Art Library

PARISIAN painter and renowned Cubist, Picabia was at first influenced by Matisse's Fauvism but progressed through most of the twentieth century's radical movements in art, including Futurism, Dada, and Surrealism. His eclectic style oscillated constantly between figurative and abstract representation. His early Cubist work is bright and colourful, unlike the sombre monotone paintings of Braque and Picasso, probably as a result of his early interest in Matisse's work. Picabia was a close friend of Marcel Duchamp (1887–1968), a pioneer in the use of ready-made art. His interest in Cubism led to a rejection of the traditional depiction of three-dimensional space, and he developed this approach in his famous series of 'transparencies', which featured a series of photographic-

style overlays of images to show a figure from a variety of viewpoints. After a brief flirtation with Orphism (a sub-group of Cubism), Picabia joined the European Dada movement, which made a radical bid to sabotage middle-class values through nihilism, mad lyricism and crazy humour. He was responsible for introducing Dada to New York, where he published two Dada magazines, *291* and *391*. In common with other Dadaists, he switched his allegiance to Surrealism, after which he produced such pieces as this bizarre construction of a tightly confined space – intended as a visual pun on the constraining influence of love.

 Portrait of a Doctor, Conversation I, Here, This is Stieglitz

CUBIST

Juan Gris (1887–1927)

Guitar and Newspaper
Daniel Malingue Gallery, Paris. Courtesy of the Bridgeman Art Library

JUAN GRIS was born in Madrid, where he studied engineering before moving to Paris in 1906. There he rented one of the Bateau-Lavoir studios in Montmartre, close to fellow Spaniard and Cubist pioneer Picasso. Gris began his artistic career by producing drawings but was painting seriously by 1910. When Picasso's celebrated art dealer Daniel-Henri Kahnweiler (1884–1976) began selling Gris' works in 1911, his artistic future was confirmed.

His heavily analytical, mainly still-life Cubist works are notable for their purity and lucidity. He followed Braque and Picasso by progressing into a more accessible 'synthetic' phase, in which recognisable forms were reintroduced into the world of fractured three-dimensional space. A lighter framework also meant a return to a brighter, more fluid palette, followed by the development of his monumental compositions of 1916–19. These large-scale works influenced Picasso's later monolithic nude series of the early 1920s.

Gris also experimented with polychrome sculpture, inspired by Lithuanian Cubist sculptor Jacques Lipchitz (1891–1973). In his last period Gris became obsessed with colour, as seen in *Guitar and Newspaper*, a simple work that displays a sculptural quality in its use of Cubist space. It was painted just two years before his tragically early death from asthma.

 Violin and Fruit Dish, Phantoms, The Bay

Wine and Grapes

Haags Gemeente Museum, Hague. Courtesy of the Bridgeman Art Library

CUBIST pioneer Braque studied fine art in Le Havre, where he met Raoul Dufy. They moved to Paris to study, where Braque was influenced by the Fauves after witnessing their Salon d'Automne exhibition in 1905. He saw Cezanne's memorial exhibition of 1907 and incorporated these influences with elements from Picasso's groundbreaking *Les Demoiselles d'Avignon* (1907), developing them into Cubism. The term 'Cubism' came from a comment made by Matisse about Braque's 'little cubes'. Reducing landscape and figures to sombre monotone cubic shapes, Picasso and Braque brought cubism to the limits, taking depictions of three-dimensional space and form and fracturing them into a kaleidoscope of shapes. Braque's reintroduction of lettering from newspapers and other media prevented the plunge into complete abstraction. He focused on the development of synthetic cubism, with the inclusion of patterning, stencilling and collage.

Seriously injured in the First World War, Braque returned to painting in 1917 and was influenced by the colourful style of his friend Juan Gris, as well as by Sergei Diaghilev's (1872–1929) Ballets Russes. By the mid-1920s, Picasso had moved into Surrealism but Braque continued with his Cubist work, as here in *Wine and Grapes*, in which he suggests three-dimensionality by exploring the different planes and facets of the objects.

 Composition with the Ace of Clubs, Still Life, The Day

Jacob and the Angel
Courtesy of the Tate Picture Library

NEW YORK-born sculptor Epstein settled in London in 1905. He became heavily involved in the emerging avant-garde Vorticist and Cubist movements after meeting Picasso and Constantin Brancusi (1876–1956) in Paris in 1912, where he also discovered primitive sculpture in the Louvre. Epstein founded the short-lived Vorticist movement with American poet Ezra Pound (1885–1972), British writer-artist Wyndham Lewis (1884–1957), and fellow French sculptor, Henri Gaudier-Brzeska (1891–1915), who was killed in the First World War. Indebted to Cubism and Italian Futurism, the group was concerned by the industrialisation of the modern world, and their work portrayed the harshness and barbarity brought about by mechanisation. This anti-mechanistic trend is best represented by Epstein's *Rock Drill* (1913–14), a bronze figure that is half-human and half-machine, initially mounted on a drill. After Vorticism, Epstein's output changed from images of brutal dynamism to energy-charged figures of monumental proportions, such as this beautifully carved alabaster statue. The simplicity of the figures belies their uplifting sense of spiritual grandeur. The angel crouches to lift Jacob to his feet; perhaps he is about to be roused from his dream of the ladder leading up to Heaven.

 St Michael and the Devil, Genesis, Rock Drill

CUBIST

Fernand Léger (1881–1955)

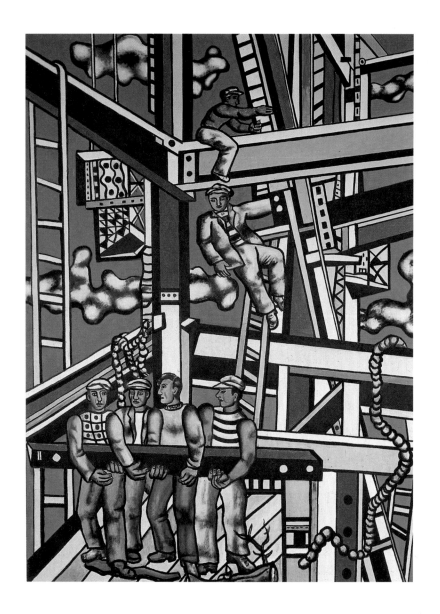

The Builders

Léger Museum, Biot. Courtesy of the Bridgeman Art Library

FRENCH painter Léger began his career as an architectural designer, later translating his fascination for construction into pioneering modernist artworks. He was influenced by Cézanne's paintings, interpreting his Post-Impressionist explorations of form as powerful and monumental blocks of colour. Léger's large tubular works have a depth that is missing in the more classically Cubist approach of Picasso and Braque. He loved urban shapes and the dynamics of city life, saying he was 'geared to the modern life'. His work demonstrates his fascination with the dialogue between representation and abstraction to redefine three-dimensional space. He was invalided out of the army during the First World War, after which he began painting working men and machinery,

intrinsic themes in much of his subsequent work. Consequently, he was allied to the Italian Futurist movement but was one of the first to progress into complete abstraction, exerting an influence on Piet Mondrian (1872–1944) and the later De Stijl movement. Although touched by Surrealism, Léger maintained a rationalist approach after coming into contact with the Purism movement of Le Corbusier (1887–1965) in the 1920s. *The Builders*, one of his later works, shows his final preoccupation with capturing objects and figures in 'free space', the tubular solidity of the men and materials contrasting with the backdrop of the open sky.

 Nudes in the Forest, The Wedding, The Great Parade

Paul Klee (1879–1940)

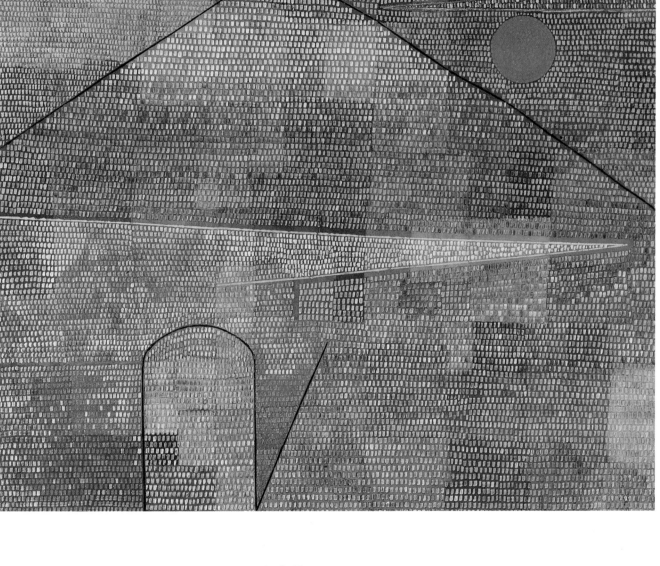

Ad Parnassum
Kunst Museum, Berne. Courtesy of the Bridgeman Art Library

KLEE'S early black-and-white graphic work revealed his expert draughtsmanship and his keen interest in Expressionism. Born in Switzerland, he studied in Munich, and joined Wassily Kandinsky's (1866–1944) celebrated *Der Blaue Reiter* group, exhibiting in their 1912 show. The influences of Robert Delaunay's (1885–1941) colourful Cubist-based Orphism movement, and a trip to Tunis in the 1910s, freed him from his severely monotone palette. As a philosopher and intellectual, Klee became a highly influential teacher at the Bauhaus Academy in Weimar in the 1920s, until his expulsion by the Nazis in 1931. Teaching alongside him were Kandinsky and László Moholy-Nagy (1895–194). The academy pioneered the integration of all artistic disciplines, advocating no

formal separation between fine, decorative and constructive arts. The teaching of design was aimed at mass production, the effects of which are still felt today. Klee's designs were sensitive to line, colour, texture and fantasy. His principles can be explained by the metaphor of a tree: the trunk represents the artist, the roots the source of ideas and forms, and the flowering the finished product. Klee's Bauhaus ideals are explored in this abstract work, which recalls the quest by the Parnassian and Symbolist groups for perfection of form as a reaction against industrial materialism.

Adventure of a Young Lady, Emerging from the Grey of the Night, The Castle in the Garden

BAUHAUS

László Moholy-Nagy (1895–1946)

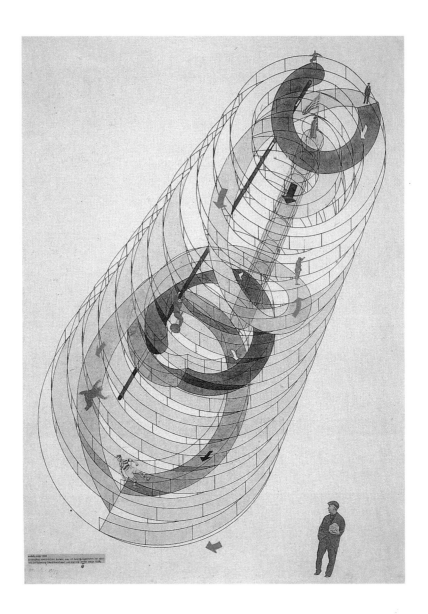

Kinetic Construction

Magyar Nemzeti Gallery, Budapest © DACS 2000. Courtesy of The Bridgeman Art Library

HUNGARIAN born Moholy-Nagy began his career as a lawyer but during the 1920s became a teacher at the highly radical Bauhaus Academy in Weimar, Germany, where he worked alongside Klee (1879–1940). He was in charge of the school's famous metal workshop. He won renown for his fantastic explorations into new sculptural media such as plexiglass, and was fascinated with the notion of construction, studying the effects of light, three-dimensional space and, importantly, movement. When the Nazis shut down the controversial Bauhaus Academy in 1931, Moholy-Nagy fled to the US, re-establishing the highly influential movement in Chicago. Through the efforts of the Constructivist group, with Naum Gabo (1890–1977) and Kandinsky he helped to create the now famous 'international functionalist style' of architecture and the industrial design style of the 1920s and 30s. Following his interest in Futurism, Moholy-Nagy became a pioneer of kinetic art, separating the notions of mass and volume by outlining form using the movement of material, and implying space with the use of light, as in his revolutionary *Light Machine, or Light-Space Modulator*. The same theme is explored in *Kinetic Construction*. Moholy-Nagy anticipated the move towards the involvement of the spectator, as introduced by installation art and the Op Art movement, in which suggested illusions are completed in the mind's eye of the viewer.

 CHX, Light Machine, Jealousy

Naum Gabo (1890–1977)

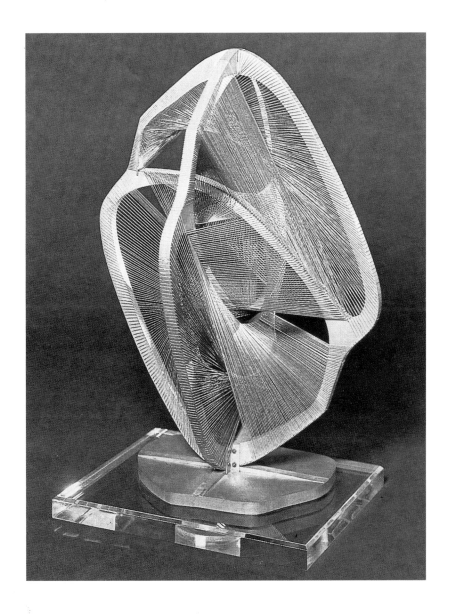

Linear Construction No. 4

The Works of Naum Gabo © Nina Williams. Courtesy of the Bridgeman Art Library

RUSSIAN-BORN sculptor Gabo trained initially as an engineer in Munich. He worked alongside his artist brother, Antoine Pevsner (1886–1962), who kept the family name, and both were heavily influenced by the Cubists. On returning to Moscow, they became involved with the avant-garde post-Revolutionary Proletariat art movement led by Kasimir Malevich (1878–1935), Vladimir Tatlin (1885–1953) and Kandinsky. The brothers wrote the influential *Realistic Manifesto* (1920), which renounced the idea of static mass as the basis for art and expounded the notions of 'rhythm' and movement in abstract work as the basis of kinetic art. When the Constructivist movement was split by an ideological battle between functionalism and more spiritual objectives, the brothers were forced into exile with Kandinsky and Moholy Nagy. They first went to Berlin and then to Paris. Gabo eventually moved to Britain, where he was highly influential on the work of Barbara Hepworth (1903–75) and Ben Nicholson (1894–1982). He then joined Moholy-Nagy's re-formed Bauhaus group in the US, where he lived from 1939. Working in glass, plastic and metal, Gabo influenced Moholy-Nagy's Bauhaus work, using light materials to show sculpture's non-static interaction with modular space. Movement and a sense of weightlessness were implied through light falling on geometric structures, as seen here in the dynamic *Linear Construction No. 4*, made from aluminium and stainless steel.

 Head No. 2, Model for Column, Head of a Woman

Vanessa Bell (1879–1961)

Studland Beach
Courtesy of the Tate Picture Library

THE daughter of Victorian biographer Leslie Stephen and sister of Virginia Woolf (1882–1941), Bell was a founding member of the Bloomsbury Group. She was one of the first women to paint the female nude at a time when women were banned from life classes. She was also an early supporter of the international movement towards Abstract art, and gained inspiration for the development of her work after she helped her lover, Roger Fry (1866–1934), to stage London's celebrated Post-Impressionist exhibition in 1910.

Bell won renown as a colourist and designer for the Omega Workshops (1913–19), which she formed with Fry, her husband Clive Bell (1881–1964), and another Bloomsbury artist, Duncan Grant. In 1916 Vanessa left her husband to live with Grant, and the couple continued a life-long collaboration, designing murals and interiors, although much of their work was destroyed during the London Blitz. The most important surviving examples of their work include their Sussex home, Charleston, now a museum.

With *Studland Beach*, Bell was influenced by Henri Matisse and Paul Cézanne and heralds Bell's progress into abstraction, with bold colour blocks and formal simplicity. The painting may be seen as an expression of the loneliness and social isolation brought about by her position as an avant-garde leader and working mother in an age when women were still struggling for the vote.

 The Tub, Mrs St John Hutchison, A Conversation

Giorgio de Chirico (1888–1978)

Piazza d'Italia

Art Gallery of Ontario, Toronto. Courtesy of the Bridgeman Art Library

ITALIAN painter de Chirico is lauded as the precursor of one of the most influential and far-reaching art movements of the twentieth century: Surrealism. He was born in Greece and later studied in Athens, Florence and Munich. De Chirico was deeply affected by the Symbolist paintings of Böcklin (1827–1901), admiring their blend of the surreal with the real. In 1917 he met Carlo Carrà (1881–1966) while recovering from a breakdown, and together they founded the Metaphysical movement.

Although the movement was short-lived, Girogio de Chirico's Metaphysical paintings mark the height of his career. They were hugely influential on Surrealist artists, who recognised in them the eloquent expression of the unconscious and nonsensical to which they themselves aspired. By the 1920s, however, De Chirico had moved to a more conventional form of expression. The Surrealists, in particular, condemned his later work, which never attained the level of success of his Metaphysical work.

The apparently random inclusion of objects in the *Piazza d'Italia* is typical of De Chirico's Metaphysical paintings. The Italian architecture was a familiar motif, as was the distant train. A sense of emptiness and vast space is apparent, and despite the inclusion of the two figures this appears a solitary, forgotten place.

The Uncertainty of the Poet, The Rose Tower, Melancholy and Mystery of a Street

Marcel Duchamp (1887–1968)

The Bride Stripped Bare by Her Bachelors, Even

Philadelphia Museum of Art © Estate of Marcel Duchamp/ADAGP Paris & DACS London 2000. Courtesy of the Bridgeman Art Library

BORN in Normandy, Duchamp trained in Paris before moving to New York in 1915. There, Duchamp met Picabia (1879–1953) and Man Ray (1890–1976), and together they founded the 'anti-art' movement Dada. Duchamp's artistic output was minimal; he was also a chess master and much of his time was taken up with this pursuit.

In 1913 Duchamp redirected modern art with his display of what he called a 'ready-made' object: simply a bicycle wheel on a stand. His theory on 'ready-mades' was that art's importance lay in the choices that an artist made, rather than in the beauty of the creation. Duchamp thought art should be intellectual, that his viewers should be mentally challenged by his art: for better or worse, both of these beliefs have flourished in modern art.

The Bride Stripped Bare by her Bachelors, Even was initially displayed unfinished – Duchamp only declared it complete in 1923 when the glass was accidentally cracked. It represents a continuation of the theme of human sexuality that Duchamp explored in earlier works. The top panel is the bride, the bottom one her bachelors. Deliberately absurd and futile, the complicated machinery does not work and the two pieces never come into contact: the implied wedding is never consummated.

 Nude Descending a Staircase No. 2, The Fountain, Bottle Rack

Georgia O'Keeffe (1887–1986)

Lake George
Private Collection. Courtesy of the Bridgeman Art Library

PERHAPS the most prominent of modern female artists, O'Keeffe was born in Wisconsin, studying art in Chicago and New York before working as a commercial artist in Chicago. By 1912 O'Keeffe had changed her career, becoming an art teacher. While teaching, O'Keeffe began to develop her notoriously unique style and by 1915 was producing stylised, almost abstract images. Without her knowledge, a friend showed her work to photographer and art dealer Alfred Stieglitz (1864–1946), who included them in an exhibition in New York. The pictures were a success and in 1917 Stieglitz put on O'Keeffe 's first one-woman show.

Following an illness, O'Keeffe moved to New York, accepting sponsorship from Alfred Stieglitz so that she could stop teaching to concentrate more fully on her art. O'Keeffe and Stieglitz married in 1923; his photographic work was a stimulus for her famous paintings of skyscrapers and enlarged close-ups of flowers.

Lake George is instantly recognisable as an O'Keeffe painting; even though it is a landscape, the focus is not on a realistic representation; the distant hill is described with her typical brevity, hinting at the form with a fluid brushstroke and intensity of colour. During the 1920s, O'Keefe divided her time between New York and Lake George.

 Sky Above Clouds, Black Iris, Jack in the Pulpit

Max Ernst (1891–1976)

The Forest

Scottish National Gallery of Modern Art, Edinburgh. Courtesy of the Bridgeman Art Library

THE German artist Max Ernst did not receive formal artistic training; instead he studied philosophy and psychology. By 1911 he had turned to art, displaying works in the Munich Blue Rider exhibitions. Ernst moved to Cologne in 1919 and, with Jean Arp (1887–1966), he founded a Dada group there. Following the success of his one-man show in 1920, he moved to Paris in 1922 and joined the Surrealist group – the artistic movement to which he was most closely allied.

Ernst made many significant contributions to the development and spread of Surrealism. Perhaps chief among these were his inventive techniques of *frottage* and *grattage*. *Frottage* employs a similar technique to brass-rubbing, producing random images that are elaborated on. Likewise, grattage is the scraping of paint from the paper, where an object beneath has raised it. These haphazard techniques enabled a form of automatic painting that followed the example set by the automatic writings of the Surrealist leader André Breton (1896–1966).

Ernst's earlier collages had combined painted images with found objects. His later works, such as his painting *The Forest*, used *frottage* or *grattage* as the starting point for bizarre, often irrational and dream-like images. Much of Ernst's work has an oppressive quality, suggesting an impending disastrous end for humanity.

 Men Shall Know Nothing of This, Oedipus Rex, Lust for Life

Sir Henry Moore (1898–1986)

Reclining Figure

Mayor Gallery, Lonodon, reproduced by permission of the Henry Moore Foundation. Courtesy of the Bridgeman Art Library

HENRY MOORE was one of the most highly esteemed and influential British modern artists, his innovative work pushing British art towards modernism. Born in Yorkshire, Moore knew at the age of 10 that he wanted to create sculptures. In 1919, following military service, Moore received a grant to study art in Leeds and in 1921 he studied at London's Royal College of Art. While British sculpture was still conventionally representational, Moore became increasingly drawn to primitive art (especially Mexican), with its greater spontaneity and freedom of form.

In the 1930s Moore's work took on Surrealist tones; while visiting Paris, Moore had admired the works of Arp (1887–1966), Miró (1893–1983) and particularly Picasso (1881–1973). It was during this 'Surrealist' period that Moore first sculpted a human figure formed from several separate pieces, as in *Reclining Figure*.

The figure is suggested rather than realistically given. It is proportionally distorted yet evokes the potential beauty and energy of the human form. The theme of the human form in repose held great potential for Moore and he returned to it frequently. Until the 1950s Moore carved his forms directly into the organic materials that he worked with – his forms emphasising and enhancing the material's qualities and vice versa.

 King and Queen, Recumbent Figure, Mother and Child

René Magritte (1898–1967)

The Human Condition II
Private Collection. Courtesy of the Bridgeman Art Library

RENÉ MAGRITTE was the co-founder of the Belgian Surrealist movement. From 1927 he lived in Paris, working with the Surrealists there for three years before returning to Belgium after disagreements between the Surrealists and their leader, André Breton (1896–1966). With the exception of some brief periods of experimentation, the style and content of Magritte's paintings was to remain unchanged throughout his career, and the artist remained true to his Surrealist beginnings. The 1950s brought a wider fame and acclaim for Magritte; as one of the most accessible Surrealist artists, he was also one of the most popular. His work has subsequently affected both advertising and Pop Art; Magritte himself worked as a commercial artist before his artwork gained recognition.

Magritte's painting style is highly polished, which gives his work an other-worldly, almost plastic, quality. Like Dalì's (1904–89) paintings, Magritte's work has recurring motifs, such as the man in the bowler hat or the fish with legs. However, Magritte's work did not centre around his own personality. Instead it is filled with visual puns, contradictory or nonsensical images and visual illusions. Magritte questioned the nature of our reality.

The Human Condition II is one of several artworks showing a painting within a painting, in which Magritte questions the relationship between art, nature and humanity.

 The Treachery of Images, The Fall, Threatening Weather

Joan Miró (1893–1983)

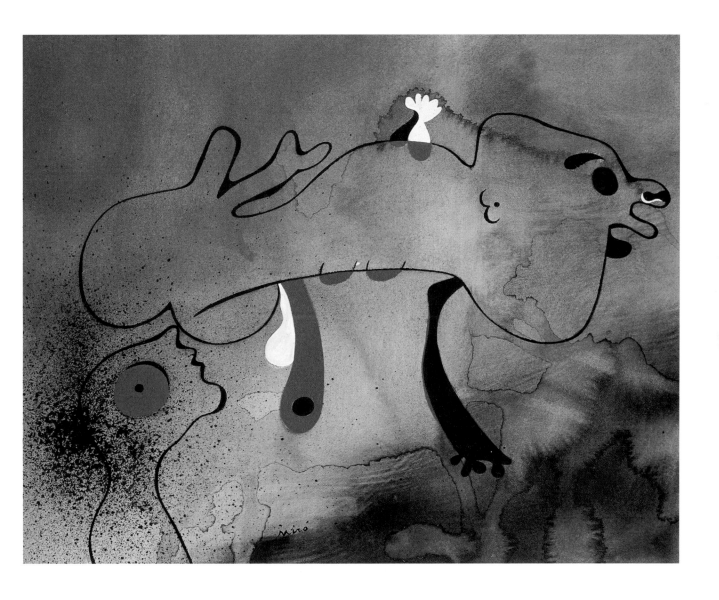

The Lovers

Private Collection. Courtesy of the Bridgeman Art Library

THE Spanish painter Miró was the son of a rich goldsmith. He originally thought of studying business but eventually chose art instead, studying in his home town of Barcelona. While living in Paris, Miró became involved with the Dada movement, before joining the Surrealists in 1924. Experimental to the last, in his late career Miró explored the fields of ceramics and stained glass.

It was probably Miró who came the closest to achieving the Surrealist goal: using chance and the unconscious as methods of exploring the 'unreal'. In much of his work, Miró employed a technique approaching automatism and his paintings are filled with psychologically pertinent symbols, amid randomly defined forms. There is often an incoherence in Miró's work that stems from his distorted, primary images, and which leans towards Abstract Expressionism.

The Lovers is produced in the style that brought Miró much critical acclaim. Like many Surrealists, Miró used a mixture of mediums; here he combines gouache, ink and paint. The barely delineated figures are just recognisably human, appearing as two bodies haphazardly melded together – as if enjoying the pleasures of sex. The figure beneath has one huge eye, emphasising the fact that it is watching the figure above.

Women and Bird by Moonlight, Harlequinade, Person Throwing a Stone at a Bird

Salvador Dalì (1904–89)

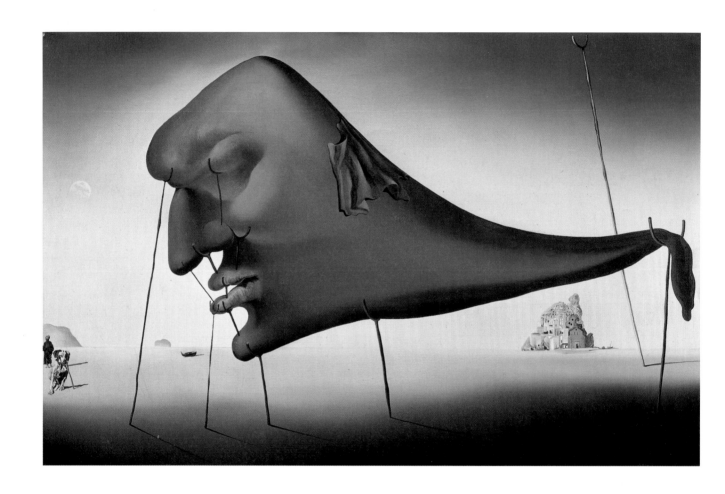

Sleep

Ex-Edward James Foundation, Sussex © Salvador Dalì-Foundation Gala-Salvador Dalì. Courtesy of the Bridgeman Art Library

OF ALL the Surrealist artists, the self-proclaimed genius Salvador Dalì became the most famous. Many critics have dismissed Dalì as a self-obsessed prankster, but his skilful technique and remarkable, often disturbing, vision left an indelible mark on twentieth-century art. Dalì was also involved in Surrealist films, and wrote books on his artistic theories as well as two autobiographies.

Born in Figueres, Spain, Dalì studied art in Madrid but was expelled from art school in 1926. Dalì returned to Figueres and there met his future wife, Gala, and leading members of the Surrealist group in 1928; both had a profound impact on his work. Dalì joined the Surrealist movement and by 1929 was incorporating highly personal, often Freudian, symbolic images into his paintings.

Dalì also explored the arena of the Surrealist object, in particular with his infamous combination of a lobster and a telephone (1936).

Sleep deals with one of the favourite Surrealist subjects – dreams. Believing that art should come from the subconscious, the Surrealists were fascinated by the creative potential of dreams – the realm of the unrestrained subconscious. Here a dismembered head, suspended with the aid of many crutches (one of Dalì's frequently used sexual images), eerily conveys the feeling of a separation from the body that occurs during asleep.

 Autumnal Cannibalism, The Persistence of Memory, Raphaelesque Head Exploding

Pablo Picasso (1881–1973)

Guernica

Reina Sofia, Madrid © Succession Picasso/DACS 2000. Courtesy of the Bridgeman Art Library

BORN in Malaga, Spain, Picasso was undoubtedly the twentieth-century's master of form. He dictated the direction of art for the first 50 years of the century and worked prolifically until his death at the age of 92.

Following his revolutionary painting *Les Demoiselles d'Avignon* (1907), he founded Cubism with Georges Braque (1882–1963), then went on to pioneer Dada and Surrealism. In later years he experimented with unique ways of seeing the world, often painting the women in his life, but never fully descended into abstraction. He lived in France, occasionally returning to Spain until the savagery of the Spanish Civil War, during which he produced this painting, his most famous work.

A powerful political statement, it was a reaction to the Nazi's bombing of the Basque town of Guernica. The monumental 14-metre (26-foot) mural represented art's condemnation of Fascism. The painting pivots around the central pyramidal structure, balanced by curves and straight lines. Picasso discarded colour to intensify the drama, producing a reportage-like photographic record. Appalling images of mutilation, death and destruction, which Picasso had explored in earlier mythological bull scenes, reach an anguished crescendo.

Night Fishing at Antibes, Weeping Woman, My Pretty

Man Ray (1890–1977)

Imaginary Portrait of the Marquis de Sade
Private Collection. Courtesy of the Bridgeman Art Library

MAN RAY was born as Emmanuel Radinski, changing his name at the age of 15 following persecution because of his obvious Russian-Jewish heritage. Born in Philadelphia, Man Ray received his artistic training at evening classes in New York, while he worked as a designer by day. In 1915 Ray met Marcel Duchamp (1887–1968) and soon became involved in the thriving Dada movement. Moving to Paris in 1921, Man Ray would later become closely associated with the Surrealist group there, contributing to their exhibitions.

Primarily remembered for his fashion and portrait photography, he also had a profound impact on modern art, more specifically in the medium of photography. In the 1920s the comparatively new field of photography was opening up as more publications wanted photographs. Man Ray and the Surrealists saw photography, like cinematography, as another artistic medium to be manipulated in pursuit of their art. He invented new photographic techniques, such as the 'Rayograph', which used the sun to bring out images of objects placed on sensitised paper.

Ray's painting, *The Imaginary Portrait of the Marquis de Sade*, is both humorous and intimidating; De Sade is solidly formed from the same bricks that have built his oppressive castle.

 The Enigma of Isidore Ducasse, Tomorrow, Gift

Dorothea Tanning (1912–to date)

A Little Night Music

Private Collection © ADAGP, Paris and DACS, London 2000. Courtesy of the Bridgeman Art Library

DOROTHEA TANNING'S only formal art training was a two-week course at the Art Institute of Chicago in 1932. In 1935 she moved to New York, working as a model while studying art in galleries and libraries. A formative influence was Tanning's visit to the New York Dada and Surrealist exhibition of 1936–37. In 1942 she met Max Ernst (1891–1976) and later became a member of the Surrealist group herself.

Her first one-woman exhibition was at the Julian Levey Gallery in 1944, where other famous Surrealists had already exhibited. Tanning and Ernst married in 1946, living in France until Ernst's death. Apart from painting, Tanning has worked as a sculptor, an illustrator, a stage designer and a novelist.

Tanning's paintings illustrate private nightmares and surreal, erotic dreams, leaving the viewer with a memorable, haunting impression. One of her most famous and successful paintings was *Eine Kleine Nachtmusik*, which shows a recurring theme of Tanning's – young girls caught up in supernatural events. The painting is erotically charged: the huge sunflower with thick encroaching vines draws the girl towards it. Behind her a sleeping girl with ripped clothes stands clutching a petal, suggesting that she has already encountered the sunflower.

 Guardian Angels, A Very Happy Picture, The Birthday

The Canal Bridge
Southampton City Art Gallery. Courtesy of the Bridgeman Art Library

WHILE many critics have dismissed Lowry as a second-rate painter primarily concerned with social comment, others view him as an imaginative historical recorder of a past industrial era. Lowry was born near Manchester, where he remained all his life.

He studied art in both Manchester and Salford, but found employment as a rent collector and clerk until his retirement in 1952. Despite his full-time work, Lowry continued to paint in the evenings and eventually had his first one-man exhibition in 1939. In 1957 a television documentary sealed his fame. With his peculiar style and familiarly gloomy subject matter, he has become one of the best-known and certainly best-loved twentieth-century English painters.

Very much an individual, Lowry stood outside the art trends of his time, choosing instead to create paintings in a 'naive' style. The many hurrying figures that crowd Lowry's industrial paintings, such as *The Canal Bridge*, are painted in an elementary, childlike manner. The figures have become known as his 'matchstick men'. By portraying his figures in such a simplistic and uniform manner, Lowry effectively suggests both the oppressive regularity of the lives of these factory workers and a callous capitalistic view of employees as dispensable human cattle.

 Coming from the Mill, The Pond, Industrial Landscape

Frida Kahlo (1907–54)

Viva la Vida

Private Collection. Courtesy of the Bridgeman Art Library

KAHLO'S renown and popularity have grown partly because of the intensely autobiographical content of her work, which reflects the intriguing details of her short life. In 1925 Kahlo was left disabled and infertile following a traffic accident; she had planned a career in medicine but this became impossible. Wracked with pain, Kahlo began painting during her recovery. In 1928 she married fellow Mexican, Diego Rivera (1886–1957), a prominent painter. Their relationship was stormy with affairs, divorce and remarriage following in later years (most famously Kahlo had an affair with Trotsky, who was later murdered in her house).

Kahlo did not have formal art training and her style of painting is influenced by Mexican folk art, so her work is termed 'naive'.

Although Kahlo is often associated with the Surrealist movement, because of the highly symbolic, hallucinatory quality of many of her paintings, she did not view herself as such.

Kahlo's subject was usually herself, and the impact of the accident upon her is illustrated repeatedly. Kahlo's last painting, *Viva la Vida*, is essentially a still life of watermelons, but their harsh, jagged shape and blood-like colour echo the themes of pain and damage in other works. Kahlo added the title just days before her death, a suspected suicide.

Self-Portrait with Thorn Necklace, What the Water Gave Me, Las Dos Fridas

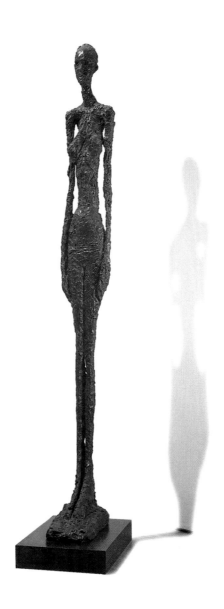

Female Standing II
National Modern Art Museum, Paris. Courtesy of the Bridgeman Art Library

SWISS sculptor Alberto Giacometti was born into an artistic family; his father was a Post-Impressionist painter, and his brother Diego was also an artist. He trained in Geneva, and then Paris, where he eventually settled. On a trip to Italy, an old man who was accompanying him died suddenly, leaving Giacometti with a lasting sense of the transitory nature of human beings, a belief that permeated his work.

Giacometti became involved with Surrealism in the 1930s but separated from the movement when he returned to depictions of the natural world – principally of the human form. He was also linked to the Existentialist movement and was a friend of the philosopher and writer Jean-Paul Sartre (1905–80).

Giacometti's most famous sculptures are the spindly, disturbingly elongated figures that he began to produce during the 1940s. These figures were inspired by the harrowing scenes of the German death camps. They illustrate Giacometti's Existentialist beliefs regarding the isolation of man: even the group figures are not closely connected, as was more typical in conventional sculpture. Instead they seem to stand desperately alone.

Female Standing II is one figure from a series created in the late 1950s. Typically, Giacommetti's female figures are shown in a stationary pose; the male figures are usually shown in motion.

 Portrait of Jean Genet, Bust of Diego, Man Pointing

SURREALIST

220

Jean Arp (1887–1966)

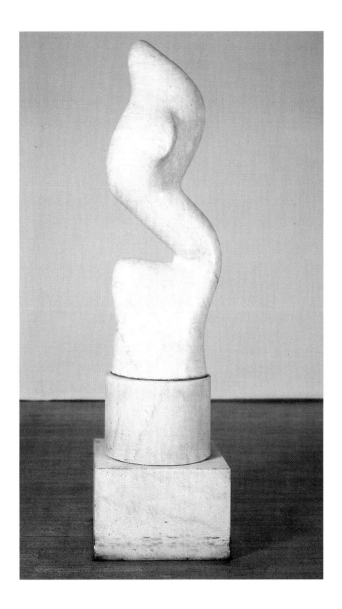

Rising Up
Scottish National Gallery of Modern Art, Edinburgh. Courtesy of the Bridgeman Art Library

FRENCH artist Jean Arp is associated with several modern art movements. In 1911 he took part in the Blue Rider exhibitions in Munich, with Kandinsky (1866–1944). The Cubist art he saw in Paris in 1914 also greatly impressed him. His quintessential artistic belief was the concept of the creativity of a freed, unconscious mind; freedom was to be found in primary, basic, spontaneous art forms. Arp was also a poet and attempted automatism (involuntary or unconscious action) in the creative process.

On the outbreak of the First World War, Jean Arp travelled to Switzerland, settling in Zurich with his future wife, artist Sophie Taeuber (1889–1943). They were both involved in the emerging Dada movement in Zurich, attending infamous 'happenings' at the Cabaret Voltaire. By 1925 Arp had moved to a town near Paris and took part in the first Surrealist exhibition. Although he retained his independence, he was closely linked with the Surrealists thereafter.

By the 1930s Arp moved away from his earlier collages, making sculptures 'in the round'. Like his collages, the sculptures are simple, abstract forms made from natural substances. The contours of his sculptures, such as *Rising Up*, flow freely, suggestive of forms found in nature. Arp's sculptures impressed the Surrealists, especially Joan Miró, and his influence is also evident in the work of Henry Moore.

 Stag, Earth Forms, Leaves and Navels

The Blue Rider

National Museum of Modern Art, Paris. Courtesy of the Bridgeman Art Library

KANDINSKY is seen as the father of abstract art. He was born in Moscow, and trained as a lawyer before turning to art aged 30. He discovered the Symbolists' interest in the occult after meeting the French Nabi and Fauvist groups during a stay in Paris, when he exhibited at the Salon of 1906.

Kandinsky became increasingly concerned with colour and reductionism of form, and briefly joined the German Expressionist group, *Die Brücke* (the bridge), who were experimenting with the linear rhythmical expression that was to become his hallmark in abstraction. The first abstract appeared in 1910.

Blue Rider, which was based around a passion for blue, is a Fauve-like work that he exhibited in his own *Blaue Reiter* (Blue Rider) show in 1911. Two earlier *Blaue Reiter* exhibitions in Munich had featured contributions from Europe's avant-garde artists: Picasso, Braque, Robert Delaunay and Paul Klee. The group were interested in the psychological power of line and colour, as applied in a primitive, child-like way but containing an inherent symbolism. The works, as here, captured drama and movement, pulsating with the energy of their explosive colour. After a brief return to Russia between 1917–20 to help inaugurate Moscow's Constructivist School of art, Kandinsky emigrated with Naum Gabo (1890–1977) to join Klee's German Bauhaus Group.

 Improvisation 26, Landscape with Church, Cossacks

Piet Mondrian (1872–1944)

Composition with Red, Black, Blue and Yellow

Haags Gemeente Museum © 2000 Mondrian/Holtzman Trust c/o Beeldrect, Amsterdam, Holland and DACS London. Courtesy of the Bridgeman Art Library

MONDRIAN was brought up in a strict Calvinist Dutch family. His father and uncle were both painters. He developed his own spiritual-science philosophy of asceticism into a powerful new art form, which he called Neo-Plasticism, in which shapes, lines and colours all have autonomous values and relationships. Using these principles, he attempted to create paintings of harmony based on an expressionless sense of order.

He studied at the Amsterdam Academy but a move to Paris in 1909 introduced him to Cubism. This resulted in his wonderful egg series (*Pier and Ocean*, 1914), in which a field of crosses creates a unity of shape, based on theosophy's symbolic belief in the egg as a signifier of the birth of the universe.

Back in Holland in 1914, he developed the *Compositions* series, in which flat rectangles of primary colours are set in a distinctive black grid. Reducing form to strict geometric shapes, he moved colours around the framework until they 'felt right'. A sense of action in apparent stillness is created within the confines of each section of the painting; the white-framed squares seem to leap out. Mondrian formulated the *De Stijl* movement in 1917, which influenced Bauhaus. On the outbreak of the Second World War, he joined Naum Gabo (1890–1977) in London, before moving permanently to New York in 1940.

The Red Tree, Broadway Boogie-Woogie, Still Life with Ginger

ABSTRACT EXPRESSIONIST

The Kiss

National Museum of Modern Art, Paris. Courtesy of the Bridgeman Art Library

PLACED alongside Picasso (1881–1973) as one of the twentieth century's major sculptors, Romanian-born Constantin Brancusi first trained as a carpenter and stonemason before studying sculpture in Bucharest. He moved to Paris in 1904, working briefly for Rodin (1840–1917) before becoming a celebrated Parisian eccentric. Fascinated, like Picasso, by African and primitive art, he was involved, along with Piet Mondrian (1872–1944), in the spiritual-based beliefs of theosophy, which led him to Hindu, Buddhist and Oriental art. This saw him radically simplifying images into universal symbols of life and fertility, although he never resorted to purely geometrical works like Mondrian's. Brancusi's strength is through simplification, as here in *The Kiss*, which was seen as a sculptural counterpart to Picasso's groundbreaking *Les Demoiselles d'Avignon* (1907) in its reduction of form.

Brancusi's sculpture heralded minimalism and affected the development of abstract art. Another celebrated piece, *Endless Column* (1920), was seen as a turning point in sculpture with its emphasis on beautifully symmetrical carving and a love of material. As British sculptor Henry Moore (1898–1987) declared, 'he made us shape-conscious.' Although he worked until his death at the age of 81, he produced only 220 works, which in later years he was reluctant to part with, simply polishing their surfaces.

 Adam and Eve, Sleeping Muse, Bird in Space

Arshile Gorky (1905–48)

Untitled
Private Collection. Courtesy of the Bridgeman Art Library

BORN in Armenia, Gorky fled to the US in 1920, leaving behind many relatives who died of starvation. He was a pioneer of the Abstract Expressionist movement; his early work was influenced by Cézanne and Picasso. He spent a long apprenticeship exploring Cubism and Surrealism, producing Synthetic Cubist paintings of interlocking flat forms within a shallow space. A series of family portraits wistfully recalled his lost past and enforced the modernist preoccupations of dislocation and alienation. An interest in Armenian myths and folklore helped to resolve Gorky's troubled past and, after meeting Willem de Kooning (1904–97) in 1933, his work began to prefigure Abstract Expressionism. He is now primarily associated with the non-geometric abstract art group of the 1940s, which was centred around New York's Greenwich Village. Influenced by Miró and Kandinsky, his work developed soft, fluid and organic shapes, as in this untitled piece from 1946. The shapes washed and spread across the canvas, anticipating the flowing aspect of Abstract Expressionism and echoing the Surrealists' interest in the irregular forms of nature. A chain of calamities that befell Gorky in the late 1940s, including a studio fire that destroyed much of his work, the onset of cancer, and a broken neck in a car crash, culminated in his suicide.

One Year the Milkweed, The Waterfall, The Betrothal II

Jackson Pollock (1912–56)

Yellow, Grey, Black

Christie's Images, London. Courtesy of the Bridgeman Art Library

WHEN most people think of Abstract Expressionism, they think of Pollock. As Willem de Kooning said, 'Pollock broke the ice'. Born in Wyoming, he eventually drifted to New York where he studied art, and also painted vast murals on public buildings as part of the WPA (Works Progress Administration) government employment project during the Depression. He was one of the few American members of the non-geometric New York Abstract Expressionist art group of mainly European exiles, but shared their experience of dislocation to an alien city. He absorbed influences from Picasso, Mondrian and Miró, and became associated with American Surrealism, contributing to the 1942 International Surrealist Exhibition. The Abstract Expressionists' concern with mythology led to his first 'drip painting' in 1947, in which form is initially non-specific but resolves itself during execution. He believed that 'painting has life of its own, which I let come through' and often stood in the middle of his canvases to work, enjoying being a physical part of the 'action painting' process. As he laid down acres of paint, often with found objects such as cigarettes and buttons embedded in it, haunting structural forms emerged from the chaotic mass, as in *Yellow, Grey, Black*, with its strong yellow- and grey-coloured armature. Pollock was married to artist Lee Krasner (1911–84). He died in a car accident in 1956.

 Going West, Full Fathom Five, Yellow Island

Willem de Kooning (1904–97)

Marilyn Monroe
Collection of R.R. Neuberger, New York. Courtesy of the Bridgeman Art Library

THE early career of Dutch artist De Kooning was influenced by Piet Mondrian's *De Stijl* movement. In 1926 he moved to the US, where he,like Pollock, became a decorator in the WPA arts project set up by government to organise employment during the Depression. The project employed 5,000 artists who concentrated on public service works such as the monumental murals by De Kooning and Gorky (1905–48).

In the 1940s De Kooning became a leading member of the New York Abstract Expressionists, a group of mainly European exiles based in New York's Greenwich Village. Their pioneering 'action art' took abstract developments into new fields, and the effects are still apparent today. Eventually the group split into two factions:

one characterised by the textural brush painting of Pollock and De Kooning; the other centred on the colour-field work of Barnett Newman (1905–70) and Mark Rothko (1903–70). De Kooning used the female form as a vehicle to balance abstraction with Surrealist-like representation in his *Woman* series of the1950s, which excited controversy because of his forceful technique of splashing paint on to the canvas. In *Marilyn Monroe*, the paint was similarly heavily applied with intense emotion. The painting is a study of beauty, twentieth-century style, exposing our modern-day emphasis on celebrity and identity.

 The Visit, Woman *series, Door to the River*

Mark Rothko (1903–70)

Blue Penumbra

Private Collection © Kate Rothko, Prisel & Christopher Rothko/DACS 2000. Courtesy of the Bridgeman Art Library

AT THE age of ten, Russian-born Rothko emigrated with his family to the US. He dropped out of Yale University to take up art. In common with other members of the Abstract Expressionist group, during the Depression he worked on the WPA art project before establishing a New York art school, 'Subjects of the Artist', in 1948 with Barnett Newman (1905–70). Inspired by Joan Miró and Surrealism, Rothko progressed into Abstract Expressionism.

Eventually Newman and Rothko formed a splinter group that concentrated on unified colour-field work and differed from the textured brush painting of Pollock and De Kooning. Rothko was particularly significant for his development of the abstract forms of luminous colour that hover like blurred horizontal mists against dramatic coloured backgrounds, as seen in *Blue Penumbra*. Such work led to critical aesthetic debate on whether the use of one colour could constitute art. Rothko believed that such paintings represented 'clarity, elimination of all obstacles between the painter and idea, and idea and observer'. Influenced by Turner's sunsets, he wanted his work to induce deep contemplation of a colour plane, which he hoped would bring the viewer in touch with their basic human emotions. The darkening palette of the late 1950s heralded Rothko's decline into depression, which led to his suicide in 1970.

 Untitled, Red on Maroon, Number 10

Be I

The Detroit Institute of Arts, Michigan © ARS, New York, DACS, London 2000. Courtesy of the Bridgeman Art Library

BORN in New York to Jewish immigrants, Newman worked in his father's clothing factory before taking up painting full time and becoming a founder member of the Abstract Expressionist movement. He gave up painting for a while in the 1940s to write art theories and establish a New York art school, 'Subjects of the Artist', with Mark Rothko.

He returned to painting, and as an existentialist, he believed art's duty was to express the terror that sprang from tragedy – he was deeply affected by the effects of the atom bombs on Hiroshima and Nagasaki at the end of the Second World War. He often used mythological and biblical themes to evoke spirituality in his paintings, and his subject matter was the 'terrible self', which centred around personal awareness rather than the subconscious world of Surrealism. His work prompted critical debate on the nature of art; like Rothko, he believed that contemplation of colour created emotional and spiritual effects in the viewer. *Be I* is a typical example of his vast, single-colour fields, which were often red and split by 'zips', or bands, as a device to open up the picture plane. The elegant *Onement* (1946) initiated this series. Newman also produced large steel sculptures, in which he developed the use of a single line in space to signify the universal chain of life.

 The Day's Residues, Onement VI, Webs V

Jasper Johns (1930–to date)

Figure Five

National Museum of Modern Art, Paris © Jasper Johns/VAGA, New York & DACS, London 2000. Courtesy of the Bridgeman Art Library

BORN in South Carolina, Johns studied at the Carolina State University, arriving in New York in 1952, where he fell under the spell of the Abstract Expressionists. His work is now seen as the critical link between Abstract Expressionism and the emerging Post-Modernist and Pop Art movement with its love of ironies, paradox and parody. Johns was influenced by Marcel Duchamp's (1887–1968) pioneering work in this field.

The choice of mundane subject matter, such as targets, numbers and the famous *American Flag* series, is a feature of Post-Modernist irony. Perhaps even more ironic is the fact that Johns' *White Flag* (1958), now in the New York Metropolitan Museum, is valued at more than $20 million.

Johns concentrated on abstract qualities of texture, colour and drawing within a representational environment, as seen in *Figure Five*, part of the 'grey number' series. His style, with exaggerated strokes and use of repetition, underlines his concern for techniques. In later work he started to combine surface collage and sculpture, as in *Field Painting* (1963–64), in which he adapted Barnett Newman's 'zip' line to include old slogans, advertising and mass media items such as coffee tins and beer cans. Such work helped to inspire Andy Warhol's (1928–87) later Campbell's soup pieces.

 White Flag, Three Flags, Field Painting

Frank Stella (1936–to date)

Agbatana II

Museum of Art and Industry, St Etienne © ARS, New York, and DACS, London 2000. Courtesy of the Bridgeman Art Library

BORN in 1936 in Massachusetts, Stella studied painting at the Phillips Academy, MA, also graduating in history from Princeton. He arrived in New York in 1959 and began to explore the new expressions of formal abstraction, developing Jasper Johns' use of repetition and flat colour work.

Pioneering early Minimalism, the young Stella strove to isolate pictorial space from that of the real world. He purged art of all metaphor and meaning, and coined the term 'non-relational' to refer to this style (it is also known as post-painterly abstraction and hard-edge painting). His early work in the 1950s tested the purity of abstraction in a controversial series of monochrome black paintings, which emphasised symmetry and the flatness of the canvas.

Later Stella progressed to 'systemic abstraction', concentrating on repetition or progression of a single element in monumental U- and L-shaped canvases. In the late 1960s he turned to brilliantly coloured semicircles – the 'Protractor' series, of which *Agbatana II* is an example – forcing the viewer to focus on the object rather than some external reality. This led to mixed-media reliefs and metal works, in which Stella challenged the boundaries between painting and sculpture. The sculpture-paintings produced in the 1980s are a wonderfully exuberant combination of forms and patterning.

 Kastura, Harewa, Six-Mile Bottom

Joseph Beuys (1921–1986)

We Can't Do It Without the Rose
Courtesy of the Tate Picture Library

BEUYS was Germany's most important post-war artist. The breadth of his vision spanned installation, video and performance art. He joined the German airforce during the Second World War, and after his plane crashed on the Russian steppes his life was saved by Tartar tribespeople, who covered him in fat to keep him warm. This incident later had a profound effect on his artistic output.

He studied art in Düsseldorf between 1946–51, when he became cathartically obsessed with images of wounding, the Cross and Madonna and Child, eventually turning to massive sculptures in fat and wax. *Tallow* and *Queen Bee* serve as emblems of his own spiritual healing. Beuys pioneered installation art, developing his 'social sculpture' theories by incorporating mundane objects into exhibits. This dislocation of ordinary objects was innovative in the developing Post-Modernist climate and influenced many subsequent artists working in installation art.

He is perhaps best-known for his pioneering performance art, which he began in 1962. Wearing his trademark fedora hat, he examined the nature of character and ritual using images from natural history and mythology. These works were captured on film and photograph, as here, the rose undoubtedly symbolising love. He was a profound believer in the power of intuition and the shaman-artist's healing powers through art.

 Tallow, Queen Bee, Felt Suit

Donald Judd (1928–94)

Untitled (copper, enamel and aluminium)
Courtesy of the Tate Picture Library

BORN in Missouri, Judd was a veteran of the Korean War who returned to study philosophy at Columbia, then began painting at the Art Students' League before completing his studies in post-graduate art history at Columbia. Dissatisfied with painting and Abstract Expressionism, he wrote papers calling for a 'new art', finally pioneering Minimalism in the early 1960s with his reliefs and free-standing structures. Judd sought to remove the artist from the creative equation and, like Stella, strove to isolate pictorial space from that of the real world. His views eventually paved the way for conceptual art and his radical simplicity affected the Minimalist design movement. He later designed furniture and architecture but disliked the word Minimalism and refused to call his work 'sculpture', believing that the term implied carving. Judd's smooth cubic and rectangular Minimalist works redefined post-war sculpture, eliminating pedestals and stressing open, weightless mass. The structures were often in beautiful metals, as in this unitled piece from 1972, or translucent plexiglass, which Judd found aesthetically pleasing. The pieces were machine-made by other people to avoid the artist's hand, recalling László Moholy-Nagy's Bauhaus kinetic constructions. Judd insisted on perfection: the mathematical precision of each work, such as the thickness of the metal or the exact placement of screws, was of primary importance.

🦊 *Untitled (1969), Untitled (1973), Untitled (1993)*

Cindy Sherman (1954–to date)

Untitled

© Cindy Sherman and Metro Pictures. Courtesy of the Tate Picture Library

BORN in 1954 in New Jersey, Sherman is a major pioneer of the feminist art movement, challenging the way in which images of women have been viewed and exploited in the arts and media.

Using her body to produce controversial photographic portraits in both black and white and colour, she parodies stereotypical images of women, challenging fashion and consumerism's empty promises. These are not self-portraits; Sherman is posing as anonymous women, with her body as the canvas. The characters are pastiches of film starlets from the 1950s and 60s (who were exploited to reinforce ideals of beauty), TV stars, or faces from 'girlie' magazines. Sherman also used film to make statements about art. In *Untitled Film Series*, begun in 1977, she framed black-and-white photographs showing B-movie images of women from the 1940s and 50s.

This untitled photograph from her 'Playboy' series deliberately captures a 'girlie' model's true mood; her sulky expression would not have been used, of course. Using Post-Modernist irony, she challenges fixed perceptions of identity, and includes grotesque dolls with decaying prosthetic body parts to question notions of physicality. Her work from the 1990s, such as *Untitled 1990* in which she plays *Bacchus* by Caravaggio, serves as a pastiche of art history and 'Old Master' images of women.

 Untitled No. 122, Untitled Film Still, Untitled No. 96

Jean-Michel Basquiat (1960–88)

Untitled

Private Collection © Estate of Jean-Michael Basquiat. Courtesy of the Bridgeman Art Library

BORN in Brooklyn, New York, of middle-class Puerto Rican and Haitian parents, Basquiat began his artistic life in the late 1970s as a notorious Manhattan graffiti artist, signing himself as SAMO.C (same old shit– crap). In collaboration with a friend, Al Diaz, he used magic markers to represent the young and disenfranchised. At first they worked on buildings, but soon found other surfaces, such as doors and furniture, covering them with wild, chaotic forms. Basquiat sold his paintings from a downtown tenement building and soon attracted the attention of the emerging Punk movement. He progressed into other media, such as junk assemblages, sheet metal and T-shirts. By the mid-1980s he was producing crayon and paint drawings of African mask-like faces, messages and writings on unprimed canvas. His work gained a massive cult following that persists to this day. Playing on the primitive African art influences that kick-started twentieth-century modernism, his work became the hallmark of Post-Modernism.

From his multi-racial background, he often portrayed the history of black people. In this untitled piece from 1984, in acrylic and mixed-media, he recalls Mark Rothko and Barnett Newman's work, as well as paintings by Matisse. He collaborated with Andy Warhol (1928-87) but tragically, like many of Warhol's enclave, died young from a heroin overdose.

Untitled (1986), Tabac, Untitled (1987)

Damien Hirst (1965–to date)

The Physical Impossibility of Death in the Mind of Someone Living
Courtesy of the Saatchi Gallery, London.

BORN in Bristol, Hirst became the most influential member of the British Art Group that emerged from London's Goldsmith's College in 1989. Six years later he was the controversial winner of the Tate Gallery's Turner prize, which led to instant acclaim for his work. Patronage from the wealthy art dealer Charles Saatchi (1943–to date) confirmed his success, and he won international recognition with Saatchi's *Sensation* Exhibition in 1985.

Renowned for his 'sculptures' of dead animals, Hirst has arguably turned taxidermy into an art form and questioned the parameters and morality of art. Here we see a tiger shark, one of the most dangerous creatures in the sea, preserved in formaldehyde and reduced to a passive, inanimate object, almost an object of

contemplation in its suspended state. Unsettling dissection works like *Mother and Calf* and *This Little Piggy Went To Market* question the ethical issues and responsibilities of mass-producing animals, on an industrial scale, for human consumption.

With his wry, ironic humour, Hirst represents Post-Modernism at its most daring, forcing us to re-evaluate the basic human emotions involved in love, life and death. Yet, as the title implies of this work certainly implies, Hirst believes his pieces are paradoxically life affirming.

Mother and Calf, This Little Piggy Went to Market, A Thousand Years

Richard Hamilton (1922–to date)

Just What Is It ...?

LONDON-BORN Hamilton is seen as the father of Pop Art and a major influence on subsequent devotees, including Andy Warhol (1930–87. His art education at the Royal Academy in London was interrupted by the Second World War, during which he retrained as an engineering draughtsman. An academic, he taught at the Central School of Arts and Crafts in London, and then at Newcastle University. He helped to establish the late 1950s Independent Group, whose members included artists, critics and architects. The group met at the Institute of Contemporary Arts (ICA) in London to discuss and popularise mass US culture.

Pop Art borrowed materials and techniques from other media, such as airbrushing and silk-screen effects, in a vast celebration of popular culture and the effects of the global mass media. Subsequently there was a creation of new universal icons, from household advertising names to superstars like Marilyn Monroe.

In this remarkable collage, set in a typical American TV studio home, Hamilton parodies a selection of household products, technical developments and male and female body icons from the late 1950s. Paradoxically, the real world outside the window shows a black-and-white B-movie image. Inside, the TV world is in colour – at a time when programmes were only in black and white.

I'm Dreaming of a Black Christmas, Interior II, Portrait of Derek Jarman

Roy Lichtenstein (1923–97)

In the Car

Scottish National Gallery of Modern Art, Edinburgh © estate Roy Lichtenstein. Courtesy of the Bridgeman Art Library

LICHTENSTEIN'S work focused on issues confronting modern middle-class American life, in a culture that was just beginning to feel the effects of the mass media. Born in New York City, he pioneered his hallmark pastiches of comic strip cartoons in the early 1960s. Although his work parodied contemporary culture, it also cleverly paid homage to it.

In enormous close-up frames of brash, bold colours, he reduced simple subject matter to strongly stylised patterns of graphic inventiveness, including cartoon speech balloons and exclamations such as *Whaam!* (1963). He composed the pictures from minute circles, carefully reproducing the dots associated with cheap screen-printing techniques of highly popular comic and newspaper strips. His subject matter often included the glamourised all-action heroes and beautiful blond heroines of comic-strip cartoons.

Lichstenstein's Pop Art reflections on the nature of beauty and the modern portrayal of women, exemplified by *In the Car*, were influenced by the pioneering and sardonic work of Richard Hamilton. Some of the same concerns have been superbly developed in Cindy Sherman's feminist photography. Lichtenstein was also a sculptor, and produced a stunning five-storey-high mural for the lobby of the Equitable Life Assurance building in New York.

 Whaam!, M-Maybe (A Girl's Picture), Big Painting No. 6

POP ART

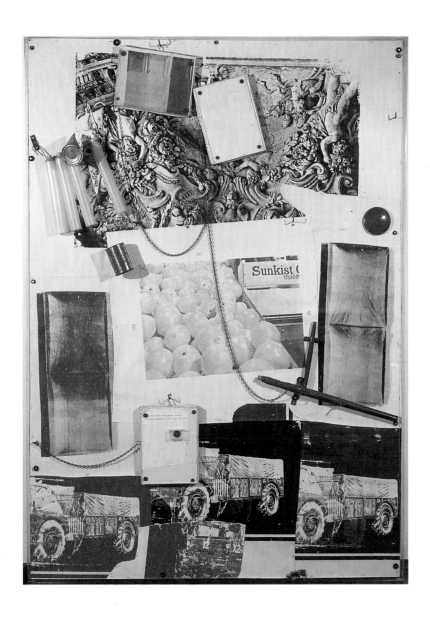

Sleep for Yvonne Rainier

Private Collection © Robert Rauschenberg/VAGA, New York, & DACS, London 2000. Courtesy of the Bridgeman Art Library

BORN in Texas, Robert Rauschenberg studied in Kansas and at the prestigious Académie Julian in Paris before travelling in Europe and North Africa. He was originally inspired by the work of the Dada and Surrealist schools before becoming associated with Jasper Johns, whose work was seen as a definite link between Abstract Expressionism and Post-Modernism and Pop Art.

Rauschenberg was a trail-blazer of the 1960s notion that anything could constitute art material, and that by harnessing the environment our perceptions of life could be challenged. Now known as 'combines' or process art, his work is a random mixture of painting, collage and ready-mades. His radical assemblages accordingly include industrial junk such as corrugated cardboard, boxes and shipping labels – a feature that has been copied by many later installation artists.

His work often incorporates silk screen prints and photographic images, as in *Sleep for Yvonne Rainier*. Because the final appearance of a piece could alter, depending on its place of installation or due to the effects of time on the materials, he draws attention to art's temporality, questioning its presumed permanence. In doing so, he re-emphasises the process of construction, a trend that was begun by the Bauhaus kinetic constructions of Moholy-Nagy and later developed by Pollock and Beuys.

 Canyon, The Red Painting, Reservoir

Campbell's Soup

A CULT 1960s figure who was associated with the hippy drug culture and emerging Punk movement, American artist Andy Warhol is regarded as the chief protagonist of Pop Art. He was also a film-maker and the manager of the famous rock band, The Velvet Underground. He worked as a commercial artist between 1949 and 1960 and, significantly, transferred these techniques into powerful parodies of consumerism and advertising.

Warhol was influenced by British artist Richard Hamilton, who pioneered Pop Art, and the Post-Modernist sculptures of Jasper Johns. Borrowing materials from other media, Pop Art studied the emerging effects of a new global mass media on popular culture, and the subsequent creation of new universal icons such as Marilyn Monroe, J.F. Kennedy and Elvis Presley, all of whom were subjected to Warhol's treatment. Painting each image by hand then screen printing them repeatedly, Warhol was fascinated by the cult of the celebrity, famously stating that everybody has 15 minutes of fame. His bohemian collective, 'The Factory', won notoriety despite several of its members, including Post-Modernist artist Jean-Michel Basquiat, dying from drug overdoses. His images, as in the *Campbell's Soup* screen print, are perhaps more famous than the original items, restating Post-Modernist questions about the ownership of an image and the process of originality.

 Triple Elvis, Marilyn Tryptich, Green Coca-Cola Bottles

POP ART

David Hockney (1937–to date)

The Board and Diver

Bradford Art Galleries and Musems, West Yorkshire © David Hockney/Tyler Graphics, Ltd. Courtesy of the Bridgeman Art Library

BORN in Bradford, England, David Hockney studied at the Royal College of Art in London between 1959–62, winning instant international acclaim for his Pop Art and modern realist work. Heavily influenced by the Pop Art of R. B. Kitaj (1932–to date), he moved to the US in the early 1960s, and is often referred to as the 'official' painter of California. During the 1960s and early 1970s he recorded the hippy era in a series of celebrity double portraits such as that of murdered fashion designer, Ossie Clark and his wife, *Mr and Mrs Clark and Percy* (1970–71).

His work captures and mythologises the romantic American dream of success and wealth. This modern diptych portrays the ubiquitous swimming pool, and forms part of a monumental series depicting the sudden or continuous movement of water. Hockney uses the cartoon qualities of bold, bright colours and strong geometric forms. The only real movement in the picture is the swimmer's exaggerated disturbance of the water, underlining the inherent tension between stasis and action. The bright Californian sunshine is defined by heavy shadows and intense blues. Hockney loved to experiment with new fabrics; this work is on coloured and pressed paper pulp. His later experiments in the 1990s employed technological developments such as faxes and photocopiers.

Mr and Mrs Clark and Percy, A Bigger Splash, Man taking a Shower in Beverly Hills

Andy Goldsworthy (1956–to date)

Sycamore Leaves
Private Collection. Courtesy of the Bridgeman Art Library

GOLDSWORTHY pioneered the Environmental Art movement, which made massive strides in the late 1990s. Born in Cheshire and raised in the Yorkshire countryside, he studied at Bradford College of Art but in his spare time worked on local farms, developing his love of the outdoors. Using nature as his medium, he regarded the land as a teacher and stimulus. Goldsworthy's influences included the monumental Land Art work of Robert Smithson (1938–73), such as *Spiral Jetty* (1970), which was constructed using earth-moving equipment. The Environmental Art movement reflected a deepening global concern about environmental deterioration and the human role in that destruction. The movement developed questions about the nature of the creative process (first introduced by Pop Art and Post-Modernism), but used nature and the weather rather than man-made detritus as its materials. Entire parks became galleries, featuring environmental displays, as here, in which stunning red sycamore leaves have been stitched together with stalks and hung from a still-green oak tree in Yorkshire Sculpture Park. Other materials used included ice, snowballs, streams, rocks and twigs. Aesthetic debate has been reopened as photography, despite its limited perspective and potential for manipulation, formed an intrinsic part of the recording of environmental artwork, the original pieces usually being fragile or transient.

 Maple Leaf Lines, Bamboo Leaves Edging a Rock, Dome of Sticks

Jeff Koons (1955–to date)

Popples
Private Collection. Courtesy of the Bridgeman Art Library

KOONS' approach to Pop Art reopened critical debate about the practice of art, ownership and authenticity at the end of the twentieth century. His works are constructed by craftspeople in factories around the world. Born in Pennsylvania, he began his studies at Maryland College of Art and then at the Arts Institute of Chicago, before moving to New York. He won celebrity status in the 1980s for his Marcel Duchamp-influenced 'ready-mades', in which he explored issues of mass media and middle-class kitsch, sentimentality and hype.

Notoriously, Koons collaborated with his Italian wife, Ilona Staller (La Cicciolina) – who famously appeared in several pornographic films – in a continuous project entitled *Made In*

Heaven (1989–91), a series of sexually explicit sculptures, paintings and posters. Koons is also renowned for his slick promotional appearances and his writing.

Popples, from Koons' 'Banality' series, which also included images of The Pink Panther and pop star Michael Jackson with Bubbles, his chimpanzee, is a replica of an internationally popular children's cuddly toy from the 1980s which was promoted across the world with a great deal of hype. *Michael Jackson with Bubbles*, a white and gold ceramic work portraying the star with a 'white' face and his pet, is a wry comment on celebrity and image.

 Puppy, Michael Jackson with Bubbles, Rabbit

Edward Hopper (1882–1967)

Chop Suey

Whitney Museum of American Art, New York. Courtesy of the Bridgeman Art Library

HOPPER was almost certainly America's most important twentieth-century realist painter. Born in New York State, he emerged in the late 1930s, bucking the trend of abstraction that was sweeping across Europe and the US. He studied at the New York School of Art (1900–06) under Robert Henri (1865–1929), the founder of the Philadelphia Realist group, and forged a purely American style, despite travelling in Europe between 1906–10. Hopper exhibited in Henri's celebrated 1913 New York Armoury Show, which was the first exhibition of Post-Impressionist and Cubist works in the US.

By 1913 a mood of melancholy pervaded his work, which intensified in later years. Paintings of empty streets, storefronts and solitary figures, often in urban settings, conjure an atmosphere of solitude and alienation. The stillness of the paintings is accentuated by their formality, combined with hard light and shadow and a focus on large, solid masses of architecture.

Despite his adherence to figurative realism, Hopper's work remained modernist in flavour. *Chop Suey* shows a representations of city life with a desolate quality, emphasised by the inclusion of an anonymous couple of women, who appear tense and unrelaxed in each others' company. The strong, eerie light focussed on them emphasises their emotional detachment from their surroundings.

 Room in New York, Windows by Night, Cape Cod Evening

The Resurrection with the Raising of Jairus' Daughter

Southampton City Art Gallery. Courtesy of the Bridgeman Art Library

ECCENTRIC British artist Sir Stanley Spencer was born in Cookham, Berkshire. Between 1908–12 he studied at the Slade School of Art in London, where Dora Carrington (1893–1932) was a contemporary. During the First World War, Spencer joined the Royal Army Medical Corps' Field Ambulance and saw service in Macedonia. After the Armistice, he executed his famous war painting, *Travoys Arriving with Wounded at a Dressing Station at Smol, Macedonia* and was commissioned to paint murals of army life for the Sandham Memorial Chapel in Burghclere, Hampshire (1926–32). Painted as a modern parallel to Giotto's frescoes in the Arena Chapel in Padua, they incorporate scenes from military life and culminate in the altarpiece, *Resurrection of the Soldiers*.

Spencer's early work was influenced by Gauguin's neo-primitive paintings of Christ and angels in Breton costume. He ignored the influences of abstraction and maintained realism in his dramatic and explicit nudes, whose detailed flesh and skin tones affected Lucian Freud (1922–to date) and Francis Bacon (1909–92) in their disturbing anatomical explorations. After 1945, Spencer returned to his favourite resurrection theme in a series of large-scale religiously poetic works. *The Resurrection with the Raising of Jairus' Daughter* is a typically imaginative and detailed triptych.

St Francis and the Birds, Self-Portrait with Patricia, Resurrection of the Soldiers

Francis Bacon (1909–92)

Study After Pope Innocent X By Velázquez
Aberdeen Art Gallery and Museum © estate of Francis Bacon/ARS, New York and DACS, London 2000. Courtesy of the Bridgeman Art Library

BORN in Dublin of British parents, Bacon travelled extensively throughout Europe. He eventually settling in London, where he worked as an interior designer before taking up fine art.

Despite having no formal art training, he rose to become a central figure of the international realist scene, and his often penetrating, disturbing and perverse visions of the human form had a profound effect on the development of nude studies.

Bacon admired Van Gogh's ability to capture raw emotion in his paintings, and was inspired to create a series of similar works in which his previously subdued palette exploded in a bruisingly violent use of colour. The suicide of his boyfriend, George Dyer, preyed on Bacon's conscience; in his fascination for Greek tragedy he allowed his own furies to pursue him through nightmarish artistic visions, which were often set in modern diptych and triptych panels related by form rather than narrative.

He was also fascinated by Old Masters Goya and Velázquez, adapting his famous study after Velázquez' portrait of *Pope Innocent X* (1650) into a shocking series that incorporated X-ray visions, legs of meat and screaming faces. He often worked when drunk; his figures are a balance between chance and order, constrained by the shape of the canvas but melting into a mire of oozing colour.

 Three Studies for Figures at the Base of a Crucifixion, Portrait of Isabel Rawsthorne Standing in a Street in Soho, Triptych

R.B. Kitaj (1932–to date)

If Not, Not

Scottish National Gallery of Modern Art, Edinburgh. Courtesy of the Bridgeman Art Library

BORN in Cleveland, Ohio and working mainly in Britain, Kitaj was briefly a merchant seaman, travelling the world before studying at Vienna's Art Academy and then at the Oxford Ruskin School (1957–59). In 1960 he attended the RCA in London, where he met David Hockney, who absorbed the influences of Kitaj in his own love of the figurative tradition.

A teacher at various times in many of the world's most renowned art schools, Kitaj's work is rich in literary and scholarly references, drawing on sources from the Old Masters to twentieth-century artists, particularly the works of Matisse and Degas.

Drawing on his Jewish heritage in the tragic aftermath of the Holocaust, Kitaj explores both the political and the social effects of contemporary mass culture, often with reference to historical events and their subsequent manipulation by the media, which is rife in the late-twentieth century. *If Not, Not* is a subtle parody combining Matisse's *Bonheur du Vivre* (1905–6), Gauguin's symbolic *Vision after the Sermon* (1888) and his Tahitian work *Where do We Come From? ...* (1887), in which memorable figures have been adapted to Kitaj's own discourse on modern war – possibly Vietnam. His haunting works of heavy symbolism and stunning lighting, often executed in pastels, become rewarding on reflection as layers of meaning begin to surface.

The Wedding, Cecil Court, London WC2, Little Slum Picture

Lucian Freud (1922–to date)

Night Portrait
Private Collection. Courtesy of the Bridgeman Art Library

THE Berlin-born grandson of famous psychoanalyst Sigmund Freud (1856–1939), British painter Lucian Freud is a modern innovator in the twentieth-century school of representational realism. His approach to the nude is to strip bare his sitter, both physically and psychologically, resulting in piercing works that reveal every nuance of flesh and skin tone. Until the late 1950s he concentrated on a hard, linear realism but a switch from sable to hog brushes meant that his portraits became more sculptural and were imbued with greater expressive qualities through the heavier application of oils.

The sculptural quality of Freud's work is evident here in the superbly painted bed cover, which has an almost tangible quality.

In contrast, the mercilessly scrutinised female nude is exposed at her most intimate, and the deployment of hard grey-blues within the skin tones is suggestive of a corpse. This technique, which is highly reminiscent of Francis Bacon's work, gives the painting a psychological intensity that has become a feature of the work of late twentieth-century Realists. In the Post-Modernist tradition, such artists challenge our fixed perceptions of existence and physicality at a time when science is also probing into the body's genetic make-up, dissecting the nature of human existence.

 Girl with a White Dog, Standing by the Rags, Naked Man with His Friend

Rachel Whiteread (1963–to date)

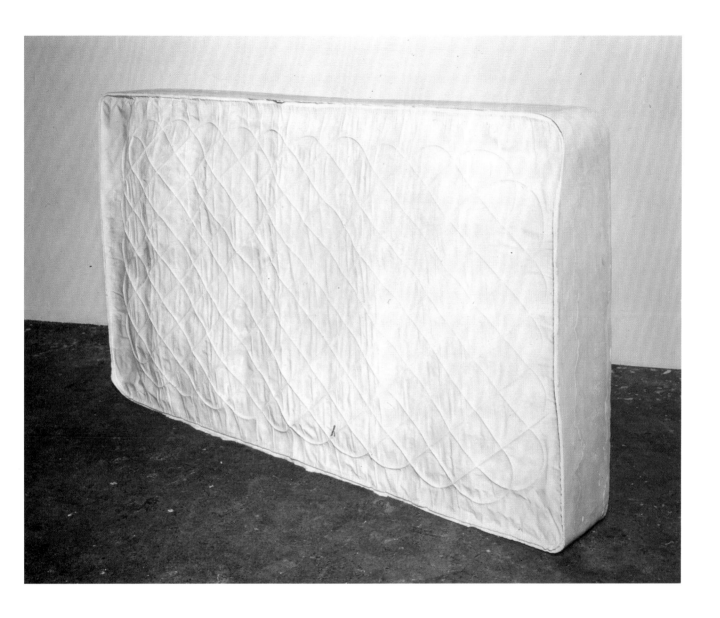

Untitled (Freestanding Bed)
Southampton City Art Gallery. Courtesy of the Bridgeman Art Library

LONDON-BORN artist Rachel Whiteread is one of art collector Charles Saatchi's most famous protégées. She won international acclaim for her sculptural work, in which familiar objects are irreverently cast in life-size forms as monuments to everyday life. In *Ghost* (1990) a whole room from a Victorian house was cast in plaster, with its contours turned inside out in the manner of a photographic negative image, leaving fossil-like traces of the windows, mantelpiece and door.

Whiteread then moved on to cast a derelict house in concrete on its original site in the East End of London. Its features were turned inside out to create another bizarre 'negative' of the entire building, which took on the appearance of a massive sarcophagus to memory, time and life; it was as though time and space were suspended in concrete. *House* won the prestigious Turner Prize in 1993 but, despite much protest, the building was demolished by the local authorities three months later.

Her ingenious works challenge our fixed notions of time and space, and force us to re-evaluate art's traditional handling of such concepts. By dislocating objects from their usual contexts, as in this untitled work, and casting them in plaster, doors, sinks, baths and beds achieve artistic status, taking on another existence as non-functional items.

 Ghost, Bath, House

Glossary of Movements

Abstract Expressionist:
An American movement of the 1940s and 50s, its most famous proponents were Pollock, de Kooning and Rothko. With roots in Surrealism, it attempted to break from Europe and tradition.

Ancient Art:
With few remaining examples, early art often favoured drawing over colour. Much surviving work was found in recently discovered tombs, such as Egyptian frescos, or recovered pottery and metalwork.

Art Nouveau:
A European and American movement, specifically of applied art, of the nineteenth century that is characterised by sinuous lines and stylised natural forms. Famous artists include Gaud', Mucha and Charles Rennie Mackintosh.

Baroque:
A period starting in the seventeenth century where the artistic style of the same name flourished in Europe. This highly ornamented style was concerned with balance and harmony of the whole work.

Bauhaus:
German school founded in 1919 to raise the profile of crafts to that of the fine art. It established a relationship between design and industry and influenced the teaching of art.

Bloomsbuty Group
Meeting in the Bloomsbury area of London in the early twentieth century, this group of artists and writers had no common philosophy. Rather, they were an intellectual elite reacting against the restrictions of Victorian Britain.

Byzantine:
Art relating to this eastern Roman Empire established in the fourth century. A religious art, it is characterised by massive domes, rounded arches and mosaics.

Classical Art:
Relating to or in the form of ancient Roman and Greek art and architecture. Primarily concerned with geometry and symmetry instead of individual expression.

Cubist:
An abstract form of art, developed in Europe in the 1900s by Picasso and Braque. It abandoned realistic representation of perspective and subject and concentrated on solidity and volume.

Early Medieval:
A highly religious art from the period beginning in the fifth century in western Europe. Characterised by iconography and paintings illustrating scenes from the bible.

Early Renaissance:
Beginning in the fourteenth century in Italy, this period attempted to emulate classical art's concern with symmetry and naturalism, searching for the perfect form.

Expressionist:
German movement of the early twentieth century that concentrated on painting emotions rather than physical reality. Bright colours and strange forms are typical in such works.

Fauvist:
From the French for 'Wild Beast', this early twentieth century style is characterised by strong colours and expressive brushwork which convey an emotional and fantastical depth.

Flemish Baroque:
Spain and Catholicism influenced seventeenth-century Flanders, producing works concentrating on spirituality and play of light, yet were still sensuous and colourful.

High Renaissance:
Developing from the Early Renaissance in the fifteenth century, Italian artists, such as Michelangelo and Titian, were interested in perspective and the illusion of space. They created more realistic pictures than ever before.

Impressionist:
Named after Monet's depiction of the effect of light on the French countryside in the 1860s, the group of artists were concerned with representing contemporary experience rather than historical events or the imagination.

International Gothic:
This amalgamation of Northern European and Italian styles was fashionable in the late fourteenth century and is characterised by elegance and an interest in detail.

Mannerist:
A reaction against the harmony and order of sixteenth-century art, typified by elongated forms and dramatic movement.

Modern Realist:
This late twentieth century American and British movement was influenced by consummerism, often reproducing photograph-like techniques of everyday scenes, in a colourful and glamorous way.

Nabi:
Inspired by Gauguin's use of colour, this group of Parisian artists were active in the 1890s. They were unconcerned with depicting reality, preferring the emotional use of colour and distortion.

Neo-Classical:
Influenced by the classical concern with symmetry and order and the eighteenth century's fascination with science, this European movement was fashionable during the Enlightenment.

Northern Landscape:
Paintings of Northern European countryside on a large scale, in particular the Netherlands and Germany. This genre was most popular in the sixteenth century.

Pop Art:
A movement of the 1950s inspired by advertising and consumer society, artists such as Andy Warhol and Richard Hamilton produced works reminiscent of comic strips and advertising.

Post-Impressionist:
A late nineteenth-century reaction to Impressionism, this group explored a symbolic use of strong colours and form rather than concerning itself with naturalism.

Post-Modernist:
Late twentieth-century artists challenged traditional notions of what art actually is with a variety of different works, they are always experimental and innovative.

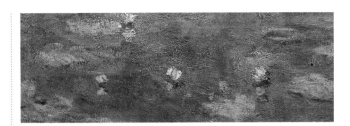

Pre-Raphaelite:
A British artistic group formed in 1848 that emmulated Renaissance painters. The subject matter was often historical or literary, and concerned itself with morality.

Realist:
Art that attempts to represent the world in an accurate or familiar way. Everyday scenes are favoured over idealised, historical or mythological subjects.

Renaissance in the North:
From the sixteenth century, the Netherlands and Germany were influenced by Italy but the 'rebirth' of their art was concerned with religious reform and ancient Christian values.

Rococo:
This eighteenth-century style is highly decorative and ornamental. Popular in France, the palette was often pastel and the subjects were playful and erotic.

Romantic:
An American and European movement of the late eighteenth century. The works were idealised and emotional rather than intellectual, laying importance on individual experience and expression.

Spanish Baroque:
The seventeenth-century Inquisition influenced Spanish art, encouraging devotional works. Mythology and still-life were also popular but painted in a dark palette.

Surrealist:
Dadaists were disillusioned and reacted against the destruction of the First World War, creating absurd anti-art. Surrealism developed from this in 1924, representing dreams and pure thought inspired by the writing of Sigmund Freud.

Symbolist:
Interested in dreamscapes and emotional, often exotic, scenes, this late nineteenth-century movement was inspired by literature. The works often use colour and line to suggest and evoke.

Glossary of Terms

Annunciation:
The moment when angel Gabriel told Mary that she was to have a son was often depicted in Gothic, Renaissance and Counter-Reformation art.

Chiaroscuro:
The contrasting effects of light and shade was employed by artists such as Leonardo and Rembrandt.

Contrapposto:
Describes the twisting torso of a figure so that they place most of their weight on one leg, much favoured by Renaissance artists.

Fêtes galantes:
Baroque and Rococo depiction of charming pastoral scenes often in a pastel palatte.

Foreshortening:
A technique which places an object to the plane of the picture making it appear shorter and narrow as it recedes.

Fresco:
A technique dating back to ancient Egypt, it involves applying pigment and water to a layer of wet plaster, buon fresco. When applied to dry plaster it is fresco secco.

Genre painting:
Most common in Dutch paintings of the seventeenth century, these paintings depicted scenes of every day life.

Impasto:
Thickly applied opaque paint which retains the brush marks.

Maestá:
Meaning 'majesty', it describes paintings and alterpieces of the Virgin and Child surrounded by saints and angels.

Mosaic:
Created by Romans, this technique involves making images by placing coloured pieces of glass and stone in cement to floors or walls.

Pietà:
Italian for 'pity'; this describes art works representing the Madonna with the dead Christ in her arms.

Sacra conversazione:
A term meaning the 'holy conversation', this representation of the Virgin and Child with saints in a separate scene was popular in Renaissance Italy.

Sotto in sù:
Meaning 'below upwards', this technique is usually associated with Baroque art. Extreme foreshortening on ceiling decoration creates the illusion of floating figures in the space above the viewer's head.

Tempera:
The most important technique for panel painting in thirteenth-century Europe until oil painting was introduced. It involved mixing pigment with water and glue.

Triptych:
Three pictures or carvings hinged together to fold and protect the central image and ease portage.

Trompe-l'oeil:
French for 'deceiving the eye', details of or paintings that have been created to trick the viewer into thinking the image is real.

Vignette:
An image that has no clear border allowing it to fade into the background.

Index of Artists

INDEX

Index of Paintings

INDEX